SPACE OPERATIONS

Air Force Doctrine Document 3-14
27 November 2006

Incorporating Change 1, 28 July 2011

This document complements related discussion found in Joint Publication 3-14, *Joint Doctrine for Space Operations.*

Cover Sheet for Air Force Doctrine Document (AFDD) 3-14, *Space Operations*

OPR: LeMay Center/DD

28 July 2011

AFDD numbering has changed to correspond with the joint doctrine publication numbering architecture (the AFDD titles remain unchanged until the doctrine is revised). Any AFDD citations within the documents will list the old AFDD numbers until the doctrine is revised. The changed numbers follow:

OLD	NEW	TITLE
AFDD 2-1	changed to AFDD 3-1	*Air Warfare*
AFDD 2-1.1	changed to AFDD 3-01	*Counterair Operations*
AFDD 2-1.2	changed to AFDD 3-70	*Strategic Attack*
AFDD 2-1.3	changed to AFDD 3-03	*Counterland Operations*
AFDD 2-1.4	changed to AFDD 3-04	*Countersea Operations*
AFDD 2-1.6	changed to AFDD 3-50	*Personnel Recovery Operations*
AFDD 2-1.7	changed to AFDD 3-52	*Airspace Control*
AFDD 2-1.8	changed to AFDD 3-40	*Counter-CBRN*
AFDD 2-1.9	changed to AFDD 3-60	*Targeting*
AFDD 2-10	changed to AFDD 3-27	*Homeland Operations*
AFDD 2-12	changed to AFDD 3-72	*Nuclear Operations*
AFDD 2-2	changed to AFDD 3-14	*Space Operations*
AFDD 2-2.1	changed to AFDD 3-14.1	*Counterspace Operations*
AFDD 2-3	changed to AFDD 3-24	*Irregular Warfare*
AFDD 2-3.1	changed to AFDD 3-22	*Foreign Internal Defense*
AFDD 2-4	changed to AFDD 4-0	*Combat Support*
AFDD 2-4.1	changed to AFDD 3-10	*Force Protection*
AFDD 2-4.2	changed to AFDD 4-02	*Health Services*
AFDD 2-4.4	changed to AFDD 4-11	*Bases, Infrastructure, and Facilities* [Rescinded]
AFDD 2-4.5	changed to AFDD 1-04	*Legal Support*
AFDD 2-5	changed to AFDD 3-13	*Information Operations*
AFDD 2-5.1	changed to AFDD 3-13.1	*Electronic Warfare*
AFDD 2-5.3	changed to AFDD 3-61	*Public Affairs Operations*
AFDD 2-6	changed to AFDD 3-17	*Air Mobility Operations*
AFDD 2-7	changed to AFDD 3-05	*Special Operations*
AFDD 2-8	changed to AFDD 6-0	*Command and Control*
AFDD 2-9	changed to AFDD 2-0	*ISR Operations*
AFDD 2-9.1	changed to AFDD 3-59	*Weather Operations*

BY ORDER OF THE
SECRETARY OF THE AIR FORCE

AIR FORCE DOCTRINE DOCUMENT 3-14
27 NOVEMBER 2006
INCORPORATING CHANGE 1, 28 JULY 2011 |

SUMMARY OF CHANGES

This Interim change to Air Force Doctrine Document (AFDD) 2-2 changes the cover to AFDD 3-14, *Space Operations* to reflect revised AFI 10-1301, Air Force Doctrine (9 August 2010). AFDD numbering has changed to correspond with the joint doctrine publication numbering architecture. AFDD titles and content remain unchanged until updated in the next full revision. A margin bar indicates newly revised material.

Supersedes: AFDD 2-2, 27 November 2001
OPR: LeMay Center/DD
Certified by: LeMay Center/DD (Col Todd C. Westhauser)
Pages: 64
Accessibility: Available on the e-publishing website at www.e-publishing.af.mil for
        downloading
Releasability: There are no releasability restrictions on this publication
Approved by: LeMay Center/CC, Maj Gen Thomas K. Andersen, USAF
        Commander, LeMay Center for Doctrine Development and Education

FOREWORD

The mission of the United States Air Force is to deliver sovereign options for the defense of the United States of America and its global interests – to fly and fight in Air, Space, and Cyberspace.

Our space forces perform functions that are critical for the joint force—intelligence, surveillance and reconnaissance; command and control; positioning, navigation, and timing; weather services; counterspace; communications; and spacelift. As our reliance on space increases, so too, must our ability to integrate space capabilities throughout joint operations. To retain the US military's asymmetric advantage based on space superiority, our Air Force must fully exploit and defend the space domain.

To that end, our space warfighters are Airmen trained in the operation and employment of space operational concepts and forces. These Airmen integrate air and space power with joint forces on a daily basis, proving their worth in military operations.

This space operations doctrine describes our shared beliefs about the integration of space power across the range of military operations. Specifically, it recommends a command and control construct for space operations we found extremely effective in recent operations. As a keystone doctrine document, it emphasizes the force-multiplying and enabling nature of space operations. It is our job as Airmen to operate and organize space forces based on the premises articulated in this doctrine.

T. MICHAEL MOSELEY
General, USAF
Chief of Staff

TABLE OF CONTENTS

INTRODUCTION

PURPOSE

This document refines general doctrinal guidance from Air Force Doctrine Document (AFDD) 1, *Air Force Basic Doctrine*, and AFDD 2, *Operations and Organization*. It establishes specific doctrinal guidance for space operations integrated across the range of military operations that extends from military engagement, security cooperation, and deterrence, to crisis response, contingencies and, if necessary, major operations and campaigns. This doctrine forms the foundation upon which Air Force commanders plan, execute and assess space operations, as well as integrate space capabilities throughout joint operations.

APPLICATION

This AFDD applies to the Total Force: all Air Force military and civilian personnel, including regular, Air Force Reserve, and Air National Guard units and members. Unless specifically stated otherwise, Air Force doctrine applies to the full range of military operations.

The doctrine in this document is authoritative, but not directive. Therefore, commanders need to consider the contents of this AFDD and the particular situation when accomplishing their missions. Airmen should read it, discuss it, and practice it.

SCOPE

This doctrine expands upon basic Air Force beliefs and operating principles found in AFDD 1 and AFDD 2, providing further detail on employing space forces and capabilities in the joint environment. Air Force forces, to include people, weapons, and support systems, can be used at the strategic, operational, and tactical levels of military operations. This document discusses the fundamental beliefs that underpin the application of space power to accomplish missions assigned by the President and the Secretary of Defense.

COMAFFOR / JFACC / CFACC
A note on terminology

One of the cornerstones of Air Force doctrine is that "the US Air Force prefers - and in fact, plans and trains - to employ through a commander, Air Force forces (COMAFFOR) who is also dual-hatted as a joint force air and space component commander (JFACC)." (AFDD 1)

To simplify the use of nomenclature, Air Force doctrine documents will assume the COMAFFOR is dual-hatted as the JFACC unless specifically stated otherwise. The term "COMAFFOR" refers to the Air Force Service component commander while the term "JFACC" refers to the joint component-level operational commander.

While both joint and Air Force doctrine state that one individual will normally be dual-hatted as COMAFFOR and JFACC, the two responsibilities are different, and should be executed through different staffs.

Normally, the COMAFFOR function executes operational control/ administrative control of assigned and attached Air Force forces through a Service A-staff while the JFACC function executes tactical control of joint air and space component forces through an air and space operations center (AOC).

When multinational operations are involved, the JFACC becomes a combined force air and space component commander (CFACC). Likewise, the air and space operations center, though commonly referred to as an AOC, in joint or combined operations is correctly known as a JAOC or CAOC. Since nearly every operation the US conducts will involve international partners, this publication uses the terms CFACC and CAOC throughout to emphasize the doctrine's applicability to multi-national operations.

FOUNDATIONAL DOCTRINE STATEMENTS

Foundational doctrine statements are the basic principles and beliefs upon which AFDDs are built. Other information in the AFDDs expands on or supports these statements.

✪ Space power should be integrated throughout joint operations as both an enabler and a force multiplier. (Page 1)

✪ Space capabilities contribute to situational awareness; highly accurate, all-weather weapon system employment; rapid operational tempo; information superiority; increased survivability; and more efficient military operations. (Page 2)

✪ Space power operates differently from other forms of military power due to its global perspective, responsiveness, and persistence. (Page 2)

✪ Global and theater space capabilities may be best employed when placed under the command of a single Airman through appropriate command relationships, focused expeditionary organization and equipment, reachback and specialized talent. (Page 3)

✪ Space is a domain—like the air, land, sea, and cyberspace—within which military operations take place. (Page 3)

✪ Space coordinating authority (SCA) is an authority within a joint force aiding in the coordination of joint space operations and integration of space capabilities and effects. SCA is an authority, not a person. (Page 13)

✪ The combined force air and space component commander (CFACC) should be designated as the supported commander for counterspace operations. (Page 15)

✪ To plan, execute, and assess space operations, the commander of Air Force forces typically designates a director of space forces, an Air Force senior space advisor who facilitates coordination, integration, and staffing activities. (Page 16)

✪ Space operations should be integrated into the joint force commander's contingency and crisis action planning to magnify joint force effectiveness. (Page 18)

✪ Integration of theater space requirements must consider both a global and a theater perspective. (Page 21)

✪ An established relationship between the CFACC and the commander, joint functional component command for space is essential to ensure flexibility and responsiveness when integrating space operations. (Page 32)

CHAPTER ONE

SPACE OPERATIONS FUNDAMENTALS

There is something more important than any ultimate weapon. That is the ultimate position—the position of total control over Earth that lies somewhere out in space. That is...the distant future, though not so distant as we may have thought. Whoever gains that ultimate position gains control, total control, over the Earth, for the purposes of tyranny or for the service of freedom.

— Lyndon B. Johnson, United States Senator, 1958

Military forces have always viewed the "high ground" as one of dominance and advantage in warfare. With rare exceptions, whoever owned the high ground owned the fight. Space assets offer an expansive view of the Earth operating high above the planet's surface; satellites can see deep into an adversary's territory, with little risk to humans or machines. Today, control of the ultimate high ground is critical for space superiority and assures the force-multiplying capabilities of space power. Tomorrow, space superiority may enable instant engagement anywhere in the world.

Space assets have not only enhanced our national security but have also fundamentally changed military operations. Because of this, the Air Force views space power as a key ingredient for achieving battlespace superiority. Space power is defined as the total strength of a nation's capabilities to conduct and influence activities to, in, through, and from space to achieve its objectives (Joint Publication [JP] 1-02, *Department of Defense Dictionary of Military and Associated Terms*). **Space power should be integrated throughout joint operations as both an enabler and a force multiplier.** This chapter focuses on space operations fundamentals, including an Airman's perspective on space power, effects-based approach to operations (EBAO), and key space operations principles.

Space operators are essential to space power, providing a uniquely persistent presence over key areas of the world through the effective employment of space capabilities. Space power arms Airmen with permanently "forward-deployed" satellites and adds another dimension to the joint force's ability to posture quickly and achieve battlespace superiority. Space power bolsters US global presence because it is not limited by terrestrial anti-access concerns. Airmen exploit this global presence and produce force-multiplying capabilities like instant global communications, timely missile warning, near-persistent surveillance and reconnaissance, and precise positioning, navigation and timing (PNT).

The ability to create accurate effects is crucial in military operations. **Space capabilities contribute to situational awareness; highly accurate, all-weather weapon system employment; rapid operational tempo; information superiority; increased survivability; and more efficient military operations.** For example, the integration of space–based PNT capabilities with airborne platforms has expanded military precision strike capabilities. Today Airmen destroy multiple targets per sortie with global positioning system (GPS)-aided munitions in all weather conditions, when similar targets in previous conflicts frequently required multiple attacks per target.

Precision based on space capabilities benefits not only weapons delivery, but is also useful to many other applications. For instance, space capabilities allow for precision in mapping terrain and environmental conditions. Airmen may collect detailed imagery and other technical characteristics of adversary assets. They can also detect and characterize an inbound missile, pinpoint its launch location, and predict its impact.

The Milstar Satellite Communications System is a joint communications satellite system that provides secure, jam-resistant communications

When applied with other forces, space capabilities increase the flexibility of military operations. Where communication lines cannot be laid, or when terrain and other line-of-sight radio frequency limitations hamper terrestrial-based communications, space communications keep forward and rear echelons in contact. In denied areas of the world, intelligence derived from space capabilities often fills critical gaps in situational awareness and operational environment knowledge. Therefore, space operations today offer flexibility through exploitation of the "ultimate high ground."

AN AIRMAN'S PERSPECTIVE ON SPACE POWER

Space power operates differently from other forms of military power due to its global perspective, responsiveness, and persistence. Through the integration of space capabilities, Airmen conduct simultaneous operations affecting multiple theaters, unlike surface forces that typically divide up the battlefield into individual, geographically-based operating areas. Because space-related effects and targeting can be global in nature, Airmen involved in the application of space power are inherently poised to accomplish an effects-based approach to space operations based on functional capabilities rather than geographic limitations.

The Air Force leverages the strengths of space platforms to produce effects based on this global perspective and responsiveness. Moreover, the space domain provides a unique degree of persistence with regard to military operations. Space assets hold the ultimate high ground; they offer the potential for persistent presence over any part of the Earth. This is a different kind of persistence than other forces provide, but it is relevant because this persistence can allow military forces to bring modern combat power to bear with a small in-theater footprint. The challenge for campaign planners is to ensure space operations are integrated throughout the joint force commander's (JFC's) scheme of maneuver across all levels of war—strategic, operational, and tactical. While this is no different than any other form of military capability, space operations usually occur over great distances and are conducted by units far from the battlefield, so the challenge is significant.

Also, the Air Force is focused on operationalizing space, which requires integration and normalization. Historically, space operations had a strategic focus. Now Airmen lead the charge to integrate space capabilities at the operational and tactical levels of military operations. Integration of space capabilities occurs within Air Force operations, with joint operations, and across the range of military operations. Moreover, the space capabilities Airmen bring to the fight are not necessarily unique; navigation aids; airborne intelligence, surveillance, and reconnaissance (ISR); long-haul communication lines; and ground-based radars provide similar capabilities. Space assets like GPS, Milstar satellite communication, and the Defense Support Program (DSP) complement existing capabilities. That is why it is important to integrate space capabilities and normalize space operations with traditional processes. The synergistic effect of combining space capabilities with traditional surface, subsurface, and airborne systems delivers persistence over the joint operations area (JOA).

However, space operations and the space domain are unique. Like mobility forces, space power defies a single model for organization and operations because it requires both a theater and a global perspective. Some capabilities create theater effects and generally are more easily deployable, and thus organize and operate within a regional model. Other capabilities have global responsibilities; such forces are best organized and controlled through a functional model. However, **global and theater space capabilities may be best employed when placed under the command of a single Airman through appropriate command relationships, focused expeditionary organization and equipment, reachback, and specialized talent.**

There are two different, but mutually inclusive, perspectives as to the doctrinal view of space. First, space is viewed as a physical domain where *space-centric* activities are conducted to achieve objectives. **Space is a domain – like the air, land, sea, and cyberspace – within which military operations take place.** This view is relevant at the tactical (e.g., operation of specific platforms), operational (e.g., synchronization of military operations to achieve the commander's objectives), and strategic (e.g., space as a domain that must be protected and controlled) levels of war. The tactical level focuses on execution of tactics, techniques, and procedures (TTP). Space is relevant at the operational level because it enables improved horizontal and vertical integration. The strategic level, consistent with national policy, is where the President of the United States (POTUS), Secretary of Defense (SecDef), and unified combatant commanders focus.

The second doctrinal view of space is an *effects-centric* view, and is particularly relevant at the operational level of war—that level at which campaigns and major operations are planned, executed, and assessed to accomplish strategic objectives within theaters. In terms of planning, execution, and assessment, commanders are concerned with achieving effects, not whether those effects come from space capabilities. The focus of EBAO is on the end result, not the differences in how individual platforms operate to achieve that result.

EBAO enables integrated space planning to achieve operational effects beyond the traditional platform-centric, attrition-based view of warfare. The tactical and operational effects obtained from space forces complement other military forces to set conditions for space-enabled warfare. The ability to produce effects through the integration of space power is key to Air Force doctrinal thought on space operations.

Also, EBAO allows for JFC direction on operational objectives while enabling warfighting components to determine the best means of achieving those objectives. If the JFC desires the effect of removing enemy air defense's command and control (C2) communications infrastructure, it could be accomplished via kinetic strike on an uplink terminal or via uplink jamming of the C2 signal. As a result, Airmen should focus on commanding air and space forces to achieve strategic and operational effects, not just on managing target lists. Recognizing the overarching role of the political sector in determining objectives, the end state, and rules of engagement, commanders must be prepared to correlate military objectives to political objectives and to advise civilian leaders on courses of action. In doing so, they should always consider the integration of all instruments of national power—diplomatic, information, military, and economic. For an in-depth discussion of EBAO, see AFDD 2, *Operations and Organization*.

Historically, the United States has enjoyed an asymmetric advantage in employing space capabilities. In the recent past, no other power or entity possessed space capabilities to match our abilities. Over the years, adversaries have changed shape and form. In the Cold War, the US prepared to fight nation states. Today, non-state actors have emerged as adversaries. Airmen have adapted to this new adversary and are employing air and space power in new ways to win the Global War on Terrorism (GWOT).

KEY SPACE OPERATIONS PRINCIPLES

This section discusses key principles and concepts to describe space operations, giving Airmen a common perspective. It includes discussion on the space mission areas, categories of space capabilities, and space-related terminology.

✪ **Space mission areas** describe the capabilities space brings to the fight. *Space force enhancement* (SFE) capabilities contribute to maximizing the effectiveness of military air, land, sea, and space operations (e.g. ISR, warning, communication, PNT, blue force tracking, space environment monitoring, and weather services).

Space control (SC) capabilities attain and maintain a desired degree of space superiority by allowing friendly forces to exploit space capabilities while denying an adversary's ability to do the same (e.g., surveillance, protection, prevention, and negation). The Air Force uses *counterspace* as an equivalent definition of the space control mission. Counterspace aligns more appropriately to other Air Force air and space power functions (i.e., counterair, counterland, and countersea), provides less ambiguity, and provides common Air Force language. *Space force application* (SFA) capabilities execute missions with weapons systems operating in, through or from space which hold terrestrial-based targets at risk (e.g., intercontinental ballistic missiles [ICBM], ballistic missile defense, and force projection). *Space support* (SS) capabilities provide critical launch and satellite control infrastructure, capabilities and technologies that enable the other mission areas to effectively perform their missions.

There are three terms used to describe different categories of space capabilities— space systems, space assets, and space forces.

○ **Space systems.** All the devices and organizations forming the space network. These consist of: spacecraft; ground and airborne stations; and data links among spacecraft, mission, and user terminals. Space systems refer to the equipment required for space operations, and these systems are comprised of nodes and links. There are three types of nodes: space, airborne, and terrestrial. Space nodes include satellites, space stations, or reusable space transportation systems like the space shuttle. Airborne nodes are primarily aircraft weapon systems that leverage space capabilities. Terrestrial nodes include any land or sea equipment that receives, processes, or uses data derived from space capabilities. Information conduits called links tie these nodes together. These links also are classified into two types: control and mission. Space operators use control links to operate space systems. Space systems disseminate data on mission links, which enable force multiplication (see Figure 1.1). For example, Airmen in the 4th Space Operations Squadron (4 SOPS) are part of the terrestrial node, and they operate and employ the Milstar constellation via the control link. The data stream between the receiver/user and the Milstar satellites in orbit is the mission link.

○ **Space assets.** Space assets include military and civil space systems, commercial and foreign entities (CFE), ground control elements, operators, and spacelift vehicles. These assets are unique in that they provide global persistence, perspective, and access unhindered by geographical or political boundaries. Military space assets are aligned under established military C2 processes, different from civil and CFE C2 processes. It is essential to integrate these separate processes for synergistic space effects.

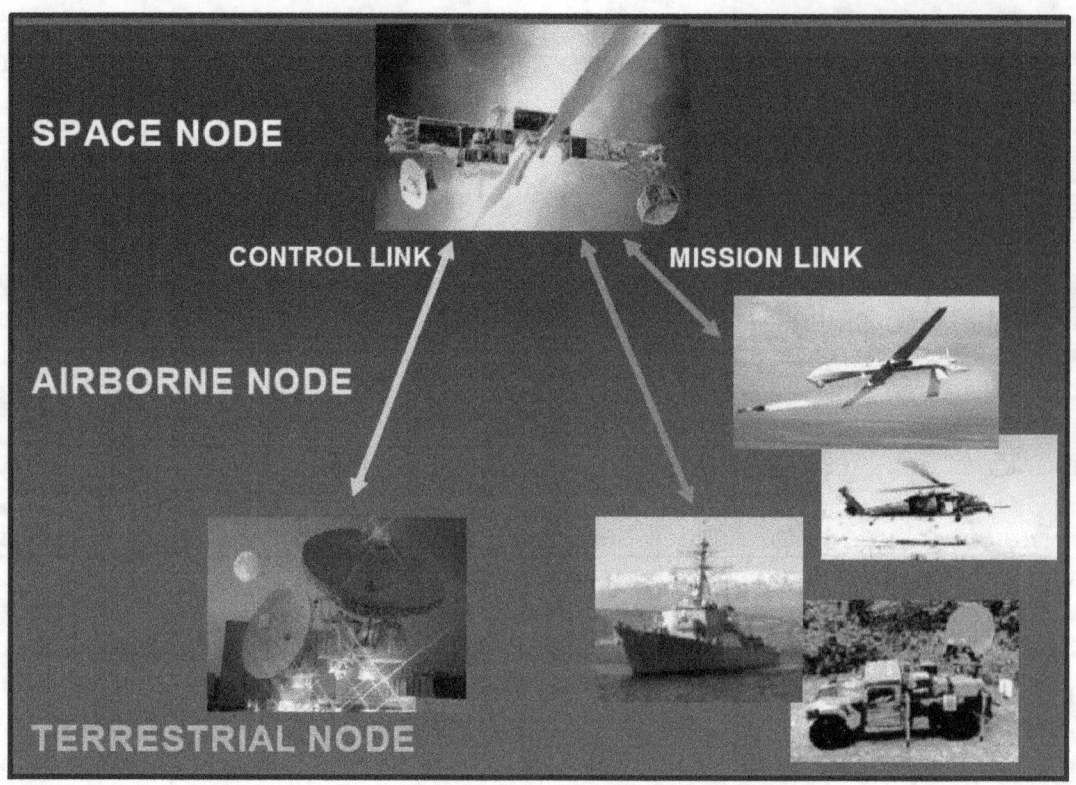

Figure 1.1. Elements of Space Systems.

✪ **Space forces.** Space forces are military space assets and personnel utilized by the joint force, are normally organized as units, and are categorized by their impact on global or theater requirements. As such, there are global space forces and theater space forces. *Global space forces* support multiple theater and/or national objectives and are controlled by the commander, United States Strategic Command (CDRUSSTRATCOM). *Theater space forces* support individual theater requirements and generally fall under the control of the geographic combatant commander (GCC). Theater space forces are primarily focused on a single theater, with little or no direct impact outside the designated area of responsibility (AOR).

Space also enables *network centric warfare* by providing a global infrastructure that can be exploited at all levels of operations—strategic, operational, and tactical. For example, a Predator unmanned aircraft (UA) depends on space for distributed operations. Space enables networking across vast distances, providing real-time horizontal and vertical integration for the warfighter. Across the operational environment, warfighters leverage space to an unprecedented degree, serving as the foundation for 21st century warfare—space-enabled warfare.

The Air Force categorizes relative advantage in the space domain by space parity, space superiority, and space supremacy. Space parity describes a *roughly equal degree* of power between friendly and adversary use of space capabilities. Next, space superiority is that degree of space advantage of one force over another that permits the conduct of operations at a given time and place without *prohibitive* interference by the opposing force. Space superiority does not mean the enemy is prevented from interfering with friendly operations, but rather that friendly losses or disruption will not prevent friendly forces from achieving objectives. Finally, space supremacy is that degree of space advantage of one force over another that permits the conduct of operations at a given time and place without *effective* interference by the opposing force. Supremacy may sometimes be an unrealistic objective because sources of space power include commercial and third party space capabilities, and it is difficult to completely deny an adversary's access to these capabilities. These categories describe the relative advantage over an adversary in the space domain.

Space forces integrate and employ at the operational level through the following organizational constructs:

○ The **air and space expeditionary task force (AETF)** is the organizational structure for deployed Air Force air and space forces.

○ The **commander of Air Force forces (COMAFFOR)** is the senior US Air Force officer designated as commander of the US Air Force component assigned to a joint force commander at the unified, subunified, and joint task force level. The COMAFFOR is the senior Air Force warfighter who exercises C2 over all assigned and attached air and space forces. The COMAFFOR commands Air Force air and space forces engaged at the operational and tactical level of war.

○ The **combined force air and space component commander (CFACC)** plans, coordinates, allocates, tasks, executes, and assesses air and space operations to accomplish assigned operational missions, when designated by the JFC.

○ The **space coordinating authority (SCA)** is an authority within a joint force aiding in the coordination of joint space operations and integration of space capabilities and effects. SCA is an authority, not a person.

○ The **director of space forces (DIRSPACEFOR)** is the senior Air Force space officer who advises the COMAFFOR/CFACC. The DIRSPACEFOR facilitates coordination, integration, and staffing activities to tailor space integration support for the CFACC.

For operations and organization of Air Force forces, see AFDD 2.

These terms and concepts describe space power and provide Airmen a common vernacular on space operations. It is important for Airmen to understand this information and articulate the impact of Air Force space operations in a joint environment. The objective is better integration of the force-multiplying capabilities of space operations.

CHAPTER TWO

COMMAND AND CONTROL OF SPACE OPERATIONS

Nothing is more important in war than unity of command.

— **Napoleon Bonaparte**

C2 of space operations is challenging due to the fragmented sources of space capabilities and the interdependence between global and theater space forces. Space capabilities come from a variety of organizations, sometimes outside the Department of Defense (DOD) with nontraditional chains of command. Also, interagency responsibilities with authority split between organizations further complicate C2 of space operations. An example involves the C2 of space-based missile warning and defense capabilities. Theater missile warning and defense during Operation DESERT STORM was performed through the cooperative use of the Air Force DSP satellites and ground radars for surface-to-surface missile launch notification to cue Army Patriot missile defense batteries. During Operation IRAQI FREEDOM, these assets were combined with the Army-Navy joint tactical ground station (JTAGS) and the Air Force's 2nd Space Warning Squadron (2 SWS) to provide missile defense warning data to the CFACC in his role as area air defense commander (AADC).

Other challenges occur when one organization owns an asset while another has responsibility for the actual operation, or when one organization operates the platform while another has responsibility over the on-board payload. For example, Defense Meteorological Support Program (DMSP) weather satellites, which provide weather data for DOD and national operations, currently fall under the combatant command of US Strategic Command (USSTRATCOM), but are operated on a daily basis by the National Oceanic and Atmospheric Administration (NOAA) under the Department of Commerce, and requirements for on-board sensor tasking are provided by the Air Force Weather Agency, an Air Force field operating agency.

Defense Support Program (DSP) provides uninterrupted space-based early warning and detection

This chapter provides a construct for C2 of space operations. Global and theater considerations are discussed followed by C2 of global and theater space forces. The chapter concludes with the CFACC's authority and role in theater space operations. This construct has proven to be effective in recent operations and exercises, and it will normally be the construct for C2 of space forces.

GLOBAL AND THEATER CONSIDERATIONS

Many space assets support joint operations in more than one geographic area. Space assets may be used to fulfill single theater, multiple theater, or global objectives. Thus, the C2 structure established for integrating space assets and forces must be robust enough to account for these various operating areas. When the effect of employing space assets meets global or multiple theater requirements, a structure that bridges more than one theater, and is capable of dealing with the non-DOD agencies, is normally necessary. In this case, USSTRATCOM usually provides such a structure.

When the effects are focused primarily on a single theater, that geographic combatant commander may control those space forces that produce strategic, operational, or tactical effects within that theater. If needed by a joint force, the combatant commander normally delegates operational control (OPCON) of theater space forces to the appropriate Service component commander and tactical control (TACON) to the appropriate functional component commander, as required. For Air Force space forces, this Service component commander is the COMAFFOR. The CFACC is normally best suited to integrate space operations within a combined/joint force. Within that force, the COMAFFOR is best suited to integrate Air Force space operations because of his ability to exercise C2 of space capabilities and the COMAFFOR's theater-wide warfighting perspective.

When the situation arises that there are no Air Force forces attached to a joint task force (JTF), the COMAFFOR to the joint force commander may be tasked in a supporting relationship to the JTF to integrate and provide space capabilities and effects. For example, multiple JTFs in US Central Command's AOR require space effects for the on-going GWOT. The CFACC provides/coordinates these effects for JTFs in Afghanistan, Iraq, and the Horn of Africa.

Although not operated or controlled by USSTRATCOM, non-military US space assets also provide critical space capabilities for warfighters. Some assets belong to national agencies such as National Aeronautics and Space Administration (NASA), National Reconnaissance Office, and NOAA. International consortia such as the International Telecommunications Satellite Organization (INTELSAT) and the International Maritime Satellite (INMARSAT) Organization own other space assets. USSTRATCOM has established coordination channels with some US non-military organizations.

If not already established, a JFC may request USSTRATCOM assistance in coordinating with these non-military organizations for integration of their capabilities. The SecDef and the combatant commanders develop processes to streamline discussions, policies, procedures, and rules of engagement for space forces. These assets are important in establishing space superiority for global and theater operations.

USSTRATCOM Joint Functional Component Commands (JFCC)

USSTRATCOM executes assigned missions through a number of subordinate elements called JFCCs in lieu of JTFs. These commands are responsible for the day-to-day planning and execution of primary USSTRATCOM mission areas: space, global strike and integration, ISR, network warfare, integrated missile defense, and combating weapons of mass destruction.

The commander, JFCC Space (CDR JFCC Space), serves as USSTRATCOM's single point of contact for military space operational matters to plan, task, direct, and execute space operations. CDR JFCC Space will conduct space operational-level planning, integration, and coordination with other JFCCs, combatant commanders, other DOD, and non-DOD partners to ensure unity of effort in support of military operations, and national security operations. CDR JFCC Space will be the primary USSTRATCOM interface for operational space effects.

The JFCC Space CDR's mission includes employing joint space forces for missile warning, PNT, communications, spacelift, and counterspace operations.

Refer to AFDD 2 for an overview of command relationship arrangements between regional and functional air and space components.

C2 OF GLOBAL SPACE FORCES

The Unified Command Plan establishes USSTRATCOM as the functional unified command with overall responsibility for military space operations. CDRUSSTRATCOM, has combatant command (command authority) or COCOM of all space forces as assigned by the SecDef in the *Forces For Unified Commands* memorandum. CDRUSSTRATCOM employs these forces to support worldwide operations.

C2 OF THEATER SPACE FORCES

Theater commanders integrate space effects throughout joint military operations. Space effects are created by a mix of global and theater space forces. Global space forces normally support national objectives and multiple theaters and produce effects for theater operations. Theater space forces move forward to conduct operations in a specific theater or consist of organic space forces assigned in theater. Global space forces and theater space forces require different command relationships and levels of coordination to achieve effects within the theater.

Space experts on theater staffs facilitate space integration. The Air Force embeds space expertise within its component and air and space operations center

(AOC) staff. Also, the Air Force augments theater staffs with additional space expertise, when requested, to assist with integration of global space effects and control of theater space forces.

Integrating Global Space Forces

When a theater requests global space forces to produce effects, the SecDef will specify a command relationship between CDRUSSTRATCOM and the combatant commander—normally a supporting/supported relationship. This will be employed at appropriate levels within both the supporting and supported commands. These support relationships fall into four categories: general, mutual, direct, and close support. *General support* is used when the support is given to the supported force as a whole. *Mutual support* is that support which units render each other against an enemy because of their assigned tasks, their position relative to each other and to the enemy, and their inherent capabilities. *Direct support* is used when a mission requires a force to directly support another specific force. *Close support* is used to describe actions by a supporting force in close proximity against objectives near the supported force which require detailed integration of the supporting actions of the supporting force. For a more detailed discussion on command relationships, see AFDD 2 and JP 0-2, *Unified Action Armed Forces*.

For space forces providing effects via a support relationship, it is important for both supported and supporting commanders to document their requirements in an establishing directive. The establishing directive should specify the purpose of the support relationship, the effect desired, and the scope of the action to be taken. Additional information includes:

✪ The space forces and resources allocated to the supporting commander's effort.

✪ The time, place, level, and duration of the supporting commander's effort.

✪ The relative priority of the supported commander's effort.

✪ The degree of authorities exercised by the supported and supporting commanders over the effort, to include processes for reconciling competing requirements and emergency events expeditiously, as required.

To facilitate a support relationship, an appropriate level of coordination should occur between the involved commanders. This facilitates planning the detailed integration of space capabilities and effects with theater operations, and enables theater warfighters to coordinate directly at either the same or differing organizational levels.

Normally, CDRUSSTRATCOM retains control of global space forces. However, a theater commander may require a greater degree of command authority than specified by a support relationship. This assumes the requisite expertise and ability to C2 exist in theater. In those instances, SecDef may transfer control over specified global space forces conducting operations affecting an individual theater.

Examples of Space Support

GENERAL SUPPORT:
During the major combat operations phase of Operation IRAQI FREEDOM (OIF), USSTRATCOM provided general support from space operations to the Iraqi theater of operations. This support relationship helped the joint force integrate space capabilities, such as positioning, navigation, and timing from GPS, and counterspace effects.

MUTUAL SUPPORT:
During the counterinsurgency phase of OIF, the combatant commander assigned the CFACC the task of space superiority. For this objective, the JFC designated the CFACC as the supported commander with other component commanders in a mutual support relationship for space operations.

DIRECT SUPPORT:
During Operation ALLIED FORCE (OAF), a direct support relationship was established between the CFACC and the 11 SWS. This relationship allowed the AOC to directly task 11 SWS personnel and exchange real-time information from the DSP satellite for time critical actions like personnel recovery after aircraft shoot downs.

CLOSE SUPPORT:
Future space capabilities will be responsive to the warfighter. These space forces may operate in close proximity with theater forces and will require detailed integration to provide close support to theater operations. These types of forces could emerge as technologies based on the Air Force's operationally responsive space and joint warfighting space operating concepts.

Theater Space Forces

If space forces are only tasked to impact a single theater, the SecDef may direct CDRUSSTRATCOM to attach the forces with specification of OPCON or TACON to the GCC with the mission requirement. As the common superior commander between the combatant commanders, the SecDef will specify the command relationship the gaining commander will exercise. The normal relationship for attached forces is OPCON, but a TACON or support relationship may be appropriate depending on the ability of the theater commander to C2 space operations, as well as other factors like the nature and duration of the operation. The GCC usually delegates OPCON of attached forces to the Service component commander who requires those forces and has the capability to C2 them. For attached Air Force space forces, this is the COMAFFOR, who also is normally dual-hatted as the CFACC, and designated supported commander for counterspace operations in the JOA. For more information on the attachment of functional space forces, see AFDD 2.

Theater-organic Space Forces

GCCs exercise COCOM of assigned theater space forces. Service component commanders are normally then delegated OPCON of those forces. During contingencies, these forces may be incorporated into a joint force. Within the joint force, the appropriate functional component commander normally exercises TACON of forces made available by Service component commanders. For space forces, this component commander should normally be the CFACC if one is designated.

Presentation of Forces

If a contingency operation requires a joint force, Air Force forces will be presented as an AETF. The commander, Air Force Space Command (AFSPC/CC) is responsible for providing Air Force space forces to an AETF, when required. Within the AETF, space forces may be attached to an air expeditionary wing, group, or squadron. Attached space forces are commanded by the COMAFFOR who commands the AETF through an A-staff and controls forces through an AOC. The AOC coordinates integration of space effects with the Space AOC/JSpOC for and execution of assigned, attached, and supporting space forces (direct liaison authority [DIRLAUTH] should be authorized for coordinated planning between AOC and Space AOC/JSpOC.)

THE CFACC'S AUTHORITY AND ROLE IN THEATER SPACE OPERATIONS

The CFACC is normally delegated SCA and designated the supported commander for counterspace operations by the JFC. In cases where the CFACC is other than an Air Force officer, the COMAFFOR will fill designated billets within the CFACC staff to ensure proper employment of space assets. If a CFACC is not appointed, the JFC may delegate SCA to the COMAFFOR, designate another component/Service commander SCA, or opt to retain SCA.

Space Coordinating Authority

Space coordinating authority is an authority within a joint force aiding in the coordination of joint space operations and integration of space capabilities and effects. SCA is an authority, not a person. As such, the commander with SCA serves as the focal point for gathering space requirements from the JFC's staff and each component commander. This provides unity of effort for space operations in support of the JFC's campaign. These requirements include requests for space forces (e.g., deployed space forces), requests for space capabilities (e.g., support to personnel recovery operations), and requests for implementation of specific command relationships (e.g., a support relationship between the CFACC and CDR JFCC Space). The commander with SCA develops a recommended prioritized list of space requirements for the joint force based on JFC objectives. The sphere of influence and focus of SCA in theater is the JOA. While a commander with SCA can facilitate nontraditional uses of space assets, planning staffs should use the established processes for fulfilling intelligence and communications requirements.

Because component commanders normally execute forces, the JFC may delegate SCA to the component commander level. Coordination should be done at the operational level because that is where requirements are prioritized to support the operations of the component commanders, which in turn support the overall campaign. Moreover, the commander delegated SCA should have a theater-wide perspective and a thorough understanding of integrating space operations with all other military activities.

SCA is a specific type of coordinating authority where authority is delegated to a commander or individual for coordinating specific space functions and activities involving forces of two or more military departments, functional components, or two or more forces of the same Service. The commander with SCA has the authority to require consultation among the agencies involved but does not have the authority to compel agreement. The common task to be coordinated will be specified in the establishing directive without disturbing the normal organizational relationships in other matters. Coordinating authority is a consultation relationship between commanders, not an authority by which command may be exercised (JP 1-02).

Responsibilities Accompanying Space Coordinating Authority

○ Recommend appropriate command relationships for space forces to the JFC or JFACC.

○ Establish, deconflict, prioritize and recommend military space requirements.

○ Recommend guidelines for employing space capabilities, such as ROE, for the joint force.

○ Guide strategy development, operational planning, and space integration.

○ Provide status of space assets that affect the JOA to key theater staffs.

○ Maintain space situational awareness.

○ Ensure optimum interoperability of space assets with coalition forces.

Delegation of SCA is tied to force assignment, and it is normally delegated to the functional component commander with the preponderance of space forces, expertise in space operations, and the ability to C2 space assets, including reachback. *Preponderance* of space forces is based on a component's space capabilities affecting the theater, through the C2 of space forces assigned, attached, and in support. Users of space capabilities are not a factor in the determination of preponderance; it is based solely on the ability to operate space capabilities and produce effects with space forces.

During times of conflict or large-scale contingencies it is important to have a coordinating authority for space within the joint force structure to appropriately represent the space requirements of the joint force. With each component and many allies having their own organic space capability, there is a requirement to integrate, synchronize, and deconflict among the space operations, redundant efforts, and conflicting support requests. By designating SCA for the joint force to a single commander, the JFC can optimize space operations in the JOA. To facilitate unity of effort within theater space operations and with global space assets, the JFC normally delegates SCA to the CFACC.

There are several reasons why the JFC normally delegates SCA to the CFACC. First, the CFACC has space expertise embedded in their staff. Second, the CFACC has the ability to command and control space forces via the AOC, including reachback to the Space AOC/JSpOC. Lastly, unlike the land or maritime component commanders who are assigned specific area of operations (AOs) within a theater, the CFACC maintains a JOA and theater-wide perspective. This perspective is essential for coordinating space operations that also support the JFC throughout the theater.

Supported Commander for Counterspace Operations and Strategic Attack

To ensure unity of command, the JFC should designate the CFACC as the supported commander for counterspace operations. These operations are designed to maintain space superiority. With US dependence on space capabilities for our asymmetric advantages in the operational environment and the proliferation of various threats to space systems, it is critical to have a single component commander focused on maintaining space superiority using all available capabilities as part of the overall joint campaign.

The CFACC is well suited to execute counterspace operations for the JFC as part of the overall campaign for several reasons: First, the Air Force has the overwhelming majority of satellite operations, maintenance, and C2 experience, making it especially qualified to plan, execute and assess offensive and defensive space activities. This expertise is integrated into the CFACC's staff. Second, the CFACC has a complete AOR perspective due to range, speed and flexibility and is able to employ various methods to attack the user/user equipment through kinetic and non-kinetic means, both directly and indirectly. Also, the CFACC, as the COMAFFOR, can recommend theater defensive measures to ensure TTPs and infrastructure reduce or mitigate potential threats. For example, the CFACC could provide guidance in the special instructions (SPINs) that units should be prepared to employ weapons in a GPS-hostile environment. Third, the CFACC, through its organic C2 centers (to include reachback) has the ability to integrate assets to deliver effects when and where needed. Fourth, the Air Force understands the treaty, legal, and policy considerations associated with space operations. For these reasons, **the CFACC should be designated as the supported commander for counterspace operations.** In this role, the CFACC has the authority to designate target priority, effects and timing of these operations and attack targets across the entire JOA (to include targets within the land and maritime AOs, although operations within a surface AO must be coordinated with the AO commander).

To coordinate with the JFC and other component commands, the CFACC may colocate an air component coordination element (ACCE) within their respective staffs. The purpose of the ACCE is to act as the CFACC's liaison to other commanders. The CFACC will normally integrate space expertise (and counterspace expertise, if designated the supported commander for counterspace) in the ACCE (or other liaison elements) to coordinate space-related issues with the JFC and component commanders, on their behalf.

In future operations and consistent with treaty obligations, assigning theater activities for force application from or through space to the CFACC would enhance unity of command. The CFACC, as the supported commander for strategic attack, would integrate these capabilities into the overall joint campaign. The CFACC has the ability within the AOC to integrate and deconflict all strategic attack capabilities to meet the JFC's objectives. All Air Force strategic attack capabilities should be integrated throughout joint operations to achieve the commander's desired effects.

Director of Space Forces (DIRSPACEFOR)

To plan, execute, and assess space operations, the COMAFFOR typically designates a DIRSPACEFOR, an Air Force senior space advisor who facilitates coordination, integration, and staffing activities. In the preferred construct of a dual-hatted COMAFFOR/CFACC, the DIRSPACEFOR serves as the senior space advisor to the CFACC in an appropriate capacity, such as special staff, to tailor space operations as part of the JFC's campaign plan. Also, this position normally requires a small support staff to work requirements specific to the JOA and ongoing military operations. Because the intended scope includes coordination with both Air Force and other Service space forces, the DIRSPACEFOR accomplishes joint responsibilities, especially given the normal situation where the CFACC is delegated SCA and designated supported commander for counterspace operations. The DIRSPACEFOR is a senior Air Force officer with broad space expertise and theater familiarity, normally nominated by AFSPC/CC and approved by the theater CFACC. AFSPC ensures DIRSPACEFORs are trained and certified to perform their responsibilities, and the CFACC provides theater-specific information and orientation.

When the situation arises that there are no Air Force forces attached to a JTF, the COMAFFOR to the joint force commander may be tasked in a supporting relationship to the JTF to integrate and provide space capabilities and effects. In the situation of multiple JTFs, the DIRSPACEFOR should work for the theater COMAFFOR/CFACC, who normally is delegated SCA, to provide space effects to the JTF based on JFC priorities.

Tasks of the DIRSPACEFOR

☯ Recommend appropriate command relationships for space forces.

☯ Establish, deconflict, prioritize and recommend operational military space requirements.

☯ Recommend policies for employing space capabilities, such as rules of engagement.

☯ Provide senior space perspective for strategy and daily guidance development, effects and target selection, and space integration throughout joint force operations.

☯ Monitor status of space forces that affect the JOA, and provide status to JFC staff and components.

☯ Maintain space situational awareness.

☯ Request space inputs from JFC staff during planning and operations.

☯ Ensure optimum interoperability of space assets with coalition forces.

☯ Execute day-to-day SCA responsibilities on behalf of the CFACC, or act as the CFACC's representative to the SCA if the authority is retained by the CFC or delegated to another component; assist the COMAFFOR with command and control of Air Force space forces if another component is designated CFACC.

The Air Force oganizes, trains and equips space forces for employment during military operations based on the construct of a COMAFFOR/CFACC. However, there may be exceptional circumstances which fall outside the bounds of this construct. First, for the rare instances when the CFACC is not delegated SCA (e.g., a JFC retains SCA or delegates SCA to another component commander), the DIRSPACEFOR will continue to work space-related issues on behalf of the COMAFFOR/CFACC. Second, for the special case when the JFC chooses to organize and employ military forces through service components and does not designate a CFACC, the DIRSPACEFOR works for the COMAFFOR, who is expected to be delegated SCA. In all these special circumstances, theater-wide coordination will be the responsibility of the component commander delegated SCA, who will normally be aided by a senior space advisor. The Air Force recommends a senior space advisor handle day-to-day SCA responsibilities on behalf of the component commander delegated SCA.

CHAPTER THREE

PLANNING FOR SPACE OPERATIONS

When blows are planned, whoever contrives them with the greatest appreciation of their consequences will have a great advantage.

— Frederick the Great

Space capabilities provide the US military the asymmetric advantages needed when projecting power worldwide throughout the range of military operations. Consequently, space assets must be considered during all phases of planning. **Space operations should be integrated into the JFC's contingency and crisis action planning (CAP) to magnify joint force effectiveness.** USSTRATCOM planning should be consistent with space-specific operations plans (OPLAN) and operations orders (OPORD) developed by the JFC. Moreover, space assets must be integrated throughout the plans developed and executed by all unified combatant commanders, including both geographic and functional combatant commanders (CCDRs).

Annexes C, N, and S of supported commander OPLANs and campaign plans contain space contributions to the overall effort. Development of these annexes is the supported commander's responsibility but requires coordinated effort between the JFC and component staffs and USSTRATCOM staffs at joint and Service component levels.

CAMPAIGN PLANNING

Combatant commanders use campaign planning to ensure orderly transition from peace to crisis and to facilitate deployment and employment of military forces. Campaign planning culminates during a crisis, but the basis and framework of a successful campaign is laid by peacetime analysis and planning. Campaign planning may begin with contingency planning and continue through crisis action planning. Military campaigns integrate air, information, space, land, sea, and special operations effects to attain national and coalition objectives. The campaign plan embodies the combatant commander's strategic vision of integrated operations required to achieve theater strategic objectives. As such, space assets should be integrated into campaign planning to ensure their optimal use.

Contingency Planning

The OPLAN serves as the foundational employment concept for a theater of operations. It provides the combatant commander's vision and intent by articulating broad operational and sustainment concepts for the duration of conflict. The resulting plan provides strategic military objectives and operational direction, organizes and tasks subordinate forces, identifies external support requirements, and designates command relationships, additional responsibilities, and objectives.

The COMAFFOR supports the combatant commander's contingency planning process through integrated theater air and space planning. This effort should be conducted as a single process rather than separate air and space processes. Theater planners normally incorporate space planning into theater OPLAN annexes. However, space requirements should be considered as part of the overall campaign, not simply limited to an OPLAN space annex. Space planning must be embedded into the contingency planning process so that space assets and capabilities are appropriately integrated into each phase of the combatant commander's campaign.

Because much of theater space integration involves forces controlled by USSTRATCOM, they need to be consulted when building plans. Reachback support may be requested to provide space-specific expertise or information to augment theater planning. Through this cooperation, theater-developed OPLANs should designate, organize, and task theater space forces and also provide realistic external support requirements for global space assets. In addition, space requirements and considerations should be included in other functional combatant commander's plans supporting theater operations.

Crisis Action Planning

Unlike contingency planning, CAP is based on emerging events and is conducted in time-sensitive situations. Planners base their plans on the actual circumstances that exist at the time planning occurs. Contingency planning supports CAP by anticipating potential crises and facilitating development of joint operation plans to facilitate the rapid development and selection of a course of action (COA). This is especially crucial for certain space operations that may need substantial coordination in advance due to their political sensitivity or because they are controlled by USSTRATCOM, civil, national, or commercial agencies. Also, one result of CAP are orders (e.g., OPORDs, fragmentary orders [FRAGOs]) that can be executed to satisfy SecDef execution direction.

Space operations should be fully integrated into the development of all COAs. A COA is a broad statement of possible ways to accomplish a mission. During COA development, as with contingency planning, planners should identify tasks for space assets in support of theater objectives. In addition, planners need to examine the role and contributions of space assets in the various phases of the campaign. During COA selection, the combatant commander should review space forces, along with air, information, land, sea, and special forces, to make an informed decision on COA selection. Additionally, global and theater space capabilities may enable the commander's situational awareness to facilitate this decision.

Range of Military Operations

Space power capabilities are adaptable across the range of military operations due to the continued presence and accessibility of space assets. Certain space assets may be applied to attain strategic-, operational-, or tactical-level effects against limited objectives as effectively as those mounted against more "traditional" wartime targets. Whether conducting space operations that shape and influence the situation or providing the eyes and ears of a sophisticated command and control system; the flexibility of space forces is integral to any operation.

Space forces provide an asymmetric advantage to military forces and operations whether responding to engagement, cooperation, and deterrence operations, contingencies and crisis response operations, or major operations and campaigns. The specific tasks involved in any given air and space operation will vary greatly, depending on the detailed context of the larger conflict or contingency, national policies and objectives, forces available to do the job, and a host of other considerations. Space capabilities may also be provided by other organizations (national, civil, commercial) throughout the range of military operations, though integration may be difficult due to command relationships.

Air and Space Operations Planning

Theater planning for space operations is also a crucial aspect to planning in order to integrate space capabilities and effects throughout the JFC's campaign. It is normally accomplished by the CFACC through an air and space estimate process that combines the mission activities and desired effects of air and space platforms into a coherent plan to support the JFC's campaign. The result is the joint air and space operations plan (JAOP). The JAOP should include the tasking of all allocated and assigned space forces and all requests for theater support from global space assets. Planned space operations that enable theater operations and produce effects in theater are captured in the JAOP. Theater space capabilities and effects derived from deployed and organic space forces under the CFACC's OPCON/TACON should be integrated through the air tasking order (ATO). The majority of JAOP development occurs within the AOC; consequently space expertise should be embedded throughout the AOC, to include strategy, ISR, combat plans, and combat operations divisions.

Joint Space Operations Plan (JSOP) Development

In concert with theater planning efforts, CDR JFCC Space plans internally for space support to the theater and to meet global space requirements. Joint space planning in support of the geographic or functional supported JFC's requirements occurs through the Space AOC/JSpOC.

The JSOP is the space equivalent to the CFACC's JAOP. The JSOP details how joint space operations will support both global missions and theater requirements. The JSOP prioritizes space operations across all AORs and functions based on geographic and functional combatant commander's requests and CDRUSSTRATCOM priorities. Theater strategists should include theater space requirements in the JAOP. Each plan should contain a sustainability assessment and delineate specific procedures for allocating and exercising C2 of global space assets. In doing so, the JSOP allows for optimum integration of global assets supporting theater operations. The Space AOC/JSpOC will use the JSOP to guide the development of the space tasking order (STO). The JSOP developed during this process should:

✪ Integrate joint space capabilities to achieve theater and global objectives.

✪ Identify and prioritize space objectives and desired effects, and the weight of effort required to achieve results in support of the theater's objectives.

✪ Indicate the phasing of space forces in relation to the theater's campaign plan.

✪ Identify and nominate adversary targets that degrade US space superiority.

PLANNING FACTORS

The following are some critical factors to consider in planning military space operations. This list is not exhaustive but serves as a starting point for air and space planners.

Phasing

Phasing provides an orderly schedule of military decisions and indicates pre-planned shifts in priorities and intent. Phasing may be used to modify the prioritization of limited space capabilities to theater operations. Space operations often occur simultaneously and can be continuous throughout the campaign, sometimes leading to a sense that phasing is less relevant to space operations. Phasing remains a useful tool to communicate the JFC's concept of operations and the shifting of emphasis between ongoing space operations. For instance, counterspace operations may be emphasized early in an operation and be de-emphasized once space superiority is firmly established. Some level of regional or temporal space superiority is likely to be a prerequisite to effective pursuit of other objectives.

Space Integration Considerations

Integration of theater space requirements must consider both a global and a theater perspective. Global integration is the responsibility of CDRUSSTRATCOM. Theater integration is the responsibility of the geographic combatant commander and the CFACC. The geographic combatant commander and CDRUSSTRATCOM normally authorize DIRLAUTH between component commanders and formalize a support relationship as the situation dictates. The CFACC and CDR JFCC Space ensure space integration occurs throughout the process. DIRLAUTH is more applicable to planning than operations and carries with it the requirement to keep the commander granting DIRLAUTH informed. For discussion on support and DIRLAUTH, see JP 0-2, *UNAAF*.

During recent warfare, including Operations DESERT SHIELD/DESERT STORM, ALLIED FORCE, ENDURING FREEDOM, and IRAQI FREEDOM, several space-related considerations have surfaced that directly impact US military success. Planners should consider the following when developing courses of action:

✪ Theater commanders should state their requirements in terms of desired effects. Deciding which space forces are required and which tactics are needed is usually best left to the supporting commander. Using support from the space-based infrared system (SBIRS) as an example, the theater may request constant vigilance (CV), a tactic used by the 2 SWS for focused warning support to a very specific geographic region. However, CV is very manpower- and operator-intensive. Very often 2 SWS can support the supported commander's request for warning with other tactics and procedures that are less demanding than CV. Theaters should not request specific tactics. Rather, theater commanders must state their desired effects.

⊙ Theater missile warning requirements should also be considered. Many factors will determine the support requirements for missile warning capabilities. Decisions on timeliness, tolerance of false reports, coverage, and data distribution may drive configuration changes in missile warning constellation alignment and possibly in the communications allocation for transmitting the reports to the theater.

⊙ Since GPS accuracy varies due to the number of visible satellites, orientation, and other factors, planners should identify AOR accuracy requirements so GPS assets can be better deployed/commanded. Specific geographical accuracy enhancements may be temporarily achieved which could possibly result in changing operational time lines.

⊙ Satellite bandwidth is another consideration, including the potential for increasing bandwidth through arrangements with commercial providers for voice, data, imagery, and video communications. Bandwidth usage is directly dependent on the amount of US access to satellite. The theater has normal processes that address these and other communication-related issues, like frequency deconfliction and restricted frequency list management.

⊙ Protected satellite communications is another consideration. Protected communications is a valuable capability that ensures secure, survivable, jam-resistant global communications to meet essential wartime requirements for high priority users.

⊙ Space-based ISR capabilities provide large amounts of data. Assessment of this data requires significant analysis by the intelligence community. Planners should account for intelligence assessments throughout the COA development process.

⊙ Combat weather assets provide the capability to forecast environmental conditions. Planners should consider the DMSP combined with meteorological information from US civil geostationary and polar-orbiting satellites. This forecast information affects military operations from timing of maneuvers to selection of targets and weapons systems. Planners should also consider potential system performance degradation due to the effect of space weather on space capabilities, like ionosphere scintillation, solar events, and meteor showers.

⊙ Planners must characterize the operational environment to include full understanding of the threats to friendly space operations. As with any campaign, appropriate knowledge of the operational environment is essential to conducting military operations. The theater intelligence directorate of a joint staff accomplishes operational environment characterization, in coordination with continental US (CONUS)-based organizations.

☼ Planners should consider integrating non-kinetic counterspace capabilities into the campaign plan. For example, some counterspace weapon systems, like the counter communications system operated by the 76th Space Control Squadron, produce temporary reversible effects such as disruption and denial of adversary satellite communications, which minimize post-conflict reconstruction of the adversary infrastructure. These systems may require frequency deconfliction, as well as deconfliction with other air, surface, information, and space operations.

☼ Theater planners must also consider friendly space vulnerabilities as well as threats. Theater planners are responsible for planning strikes on adversary counterspace capabilities or preparing alternatives for the possible loss of friendly space capabilities if strikes are neither appropriate nor feasible. Strikes may not be appropriate or feasible if the intelligence value of the adversary space capability is deemed more important. They also should consider available countermeasures. An essential part of this effort will be attack detection, assessment, and reporting. Operators and planners must know as quickly as possible the origin of any anomaly and be able to identify and geolocate the threat in a timely manner. Determining whether an event is the result of intentional attack, unintentional interference, or space weather is crucial in determining a course of action.

☼ Potential adversaries have access to a range of space systems and services. This includes fielding of potential counterspace assets (some commercially available) against US space assets. Even an adversary with no indigenous space assets may use space through US, allied, commercial, or consortium space services. These services could potentially include precision navigation, high-resolution imagery, environmental monitoring, and satellite communications. For example, during Operation IRAQI FREEDOM, the Iraqi government used a leased transponder on Arab Satellite Communication Organization (ARABSAT), a Middle Eastern consortium-owned communications satellite, to broadcast propaganda on news networks.

☼ Planners should consider targeting adversary space assets using all instruments of national power. Adversary space targets may include data links; launch sites; booster storage facilities; satellite storage and assembly facilities; mission data processing facilities; communications links; telemetry, tracking, and commanding nodes; satellites; research and development facilities; and launch vehicles. Planners should consider the potential impact of allowing an adversary unrestricted or unlimited use of a space asset. If the potential impact is sufficient enough to require action, then the desired effect (deception, disruption, denial, degradation, or destruction) should be considered. For example, if the objective is to prevent an adversary from using space imagery to observe preparations for a counteroffensive in a specific area, then any instrument of power could be employed: Diplomatic—persuade a consortia-owned satellite company to deny service to the adversary;

Informational—provide US intelligence to a friendly nation in exchange for their denial of information to adversaries; Military—denial, disruption, degradation, deception, or destruction of an adversary space system; or Economic—buy imagery to prevent the adversary from acquiring it. Additionally, if the objective is to permanently disrupt adversary C2 of fielded forces, any of the instruments of power could be effective to include permanent destruction of assets, if necessary. Planners must continuously mesh appropriate actions with respect to a target's intelligence value, JFC objective, the action's impact on conflict escalation, and collateral damage mitigation.

SPACE INTELLIGENCE PREPARATION OF THE OPERATIONAL ENVIRONMENT

CDR JFCC Space is responsible for monitoring status and capabilities of foreign space assets. The Space AOC that forms the core of the JSpOC provides the capability to operationally plan and execute operations for military space forces. Within the Space AOC/JSpOC, the ISR division conducts intelligence preparation of the operational environment (IPOE) to support operational employment of space forces. IPOE is a process involving detailed research, analysis, and knowledge of the adversary regarding topics such as force disposition, force sustainment, deployment of forces, weapon system capabilities and employment doctrine, environmental conditions, and most likely the most dangerous courses of action. IPOE consists of four phases and can readily be applied to the space mission area:

✪ Defining the Operational Environment: This involves determining the orbital and terrestrial regimes in which space forces will be employed and space effects will be generated or realized. Space intelligence planners will bound the intelligence preparation needs by using satellite assessed maneuver capabilities and ranges to determine the potential area of interest and potential natural hazards, for example, predicting upcoming meteor showers, solar flares or other significant environmental threats or obstacles to space vehicles or communications signals. This also includes determination of which nation-states are supporting or affected by a potential conflict and possible avenues of approach for friendly forces. It also includes mapping the background electromagnetic environment and characterizing or mapping the coherent signals in that environment.

✪ Describing Operational Environment Effects: Generally, space operations focus on surface, exoatmospheric, and electromagnetic dimensions of the operational environment. On the surface, the IPOE process is concerned with the effects of the environment on the ground nodes that support space operations which may include terrestrial weather conditions which inhibit or enhance space operations. In the exoatmospheric environment, predicting the effects of the space environment on adversary and third-country space capabilities might include predicting the probability of being struck by debris or meteoroids, potential space environment effects on a spacecraft, possible avenues of attack for enemy forces, and evaluating environment-based limitations on the maneuver capabilities of space vehicles.

Describing electromagnetic effects includes determining the effect of an energized atmosphere or scintillated ionosphere on space communications, determining the susceptibility of a given signal, satellite, line of communication, or ground asset to the effects of the electromagnetic environment (such as interference).

⚙ Evaluating the Adversary: This includes evaluating the adversary force composition and order of battle; satellite capabilities; offensive or defensive counterspace capabilities, tactics, and doctrine; ability to sustain or reconstitute space capabilities; the friendly assets the adversary is likely to target; and the adversary's willingness to engage in various combat operations. Additional analysis is performed on enemy space centers of gravity and critical nodes and assets that are critical to the success of the enemy's operations. Furthermore, US forces must evaluate adversary access to commercial space products and services by analyzing their impact on the battle space. US forces must also attempt to understand enemy space crew force training status, use of space communications and ISR capabilities, and C2 capabilities.

⚙ Determining Adversary COA: Intelligence analysts fuse knowledge of adversary capabilities and the environment, as well as assessments of enemy objectives and desired end state to determine potential enemy courses of action. This includes determination of most likely and most dangerous COAs. It also includes evaluation of the branches and sequels of these COAs.

Thorough and detailed IPOE is a necessary prerequisite to effective conduct of space operations. Well-accomplished IPOE provides commanders at all levels with intelligence decision aids necessary to accomplish operational objectives.

Space intelligence preparation of the operational environment is a key component of predictive operational environment awareness, thus supporting the commander's multidimensional understanding of the operational environment in time, space, and effect, regardless of the adversary, location, weather, or time of day. PBA is continuous and achieved by the commander through possession of relevant, comprehensive, knowledge, including an accurate forecast of pertinent influences in the operational environment. This knowledge of the operational environment, in concert with C2, permits commanders to anticipate future conditions, assess changing conditions, establish priorities, exploit emerging opportunities, and act with a degree of speed and certainty not matched by our adversaries.

Evolved Expendable Launch Vehicle – First Atlas V launch from Cape Canaveral AFS, FL in August 2002

SPACELIFT

Planners should be aware of the limitations of the current US spacelift infrastructure. Today, launching a satellite requires extensive pre-launch preparation and checkout followed by extensive on-orbit checkout prior to operations. In addition, the US does not have the capability to perform multiple launches in rapid succession, or make rapid changes to a planned launch's payload. Today, spacelift requirements need to be identified years ahead of operational need. Furthermore, military planners are limited to on-orbit assets when responding to contingencies.

In the future, the Air Force may field a robust "launch-on-demand" spacelift infrastructure, the ability to place a satellite on orbit within days or even hours of being requested. Combined with operationally responsive satellites, military planners will have more flexibility to meet joint warfighter requirements.

LEGAL ISSUES

The laws applicable to space operations flow mainly from four treaties. Additionally, general principles of international law, including those embodied in the United Nations Charter and law of armed conflict, apply to the conduct of space operations. There are also several arms control agreements impacting military space activities. Domestically, we must consider the impact of US laws and policies on our space activities. While the space legal regime imposes a few significant constraints, the bulk of this regime provides a great deal of flexibility for military operations in space.

- ✪ **The Outer Space Treaty.** The 1967 Treaty on Principles Governing the Activities of States in the Exploration and Use of Outer Space, Including the Moon and Other Celestial Bodies, more familiarly known as the Outer Space Treaty (OST), establishes the fundamental precepts governing outer space operations. The OST establishes several important principles:

  - ✪ ✪ **The Freedom Principle.** Article I of the OST establishes that outer space "shall be free for exploration and use by all States without discrimination of any kind...." An important aspect of this principle is that satellites may freely operate in space, including over other nations, without the same sovereignty concerns applicable to territorial airspace relating to the overflight of aircraft.

  - ✪ ✪ **The Non-Appropriation Principle.** Article II of the OST provides that outer space is "not subject to national appropriation by claim of sovereignty, by means of use or occupation, or by any other means."

  - ✪ ✪ **The Applicability of International Law.** Article III clarifies that international law applies to activities in outer space. The right of self-defense, as recognized in the United Nations Charter and more fundamentally in customary international law, applies in outer space. Also, law of war precepts such as necessity, distinction and proportionality will apply to any military activity in outer space.

  - ✪ ✪ **Weapons in Space.** Article IV prohibits placing nuclear weapons or other weapons of mass destruction in orbit around the earth, installing them on the Moon or any other celestial body, or otherwise stationing them in outer space.

Article IV also prohibits a limited range of military activities to include establishing bases, weapons testing, and the conduct of military maneuvers on celestial bodies. Thus, the placement of weapons other than weapons of mass destruction in outer space is permissible (except for testing of a weapon on celestial bodies), as is the transit of nuclear weapons, such as ICBMs, through space.

✪ ✪ **Peaceful Purposes.** The OST recognizes "the exploration and use of outer space for peaceful purposes." The majority of nations have traditionally held that the "peaceful purposes" language does not prohibit military activities in outer space; such activities have taken place throughout the space age without significant international protest. The phrase, rather, has been interpreted to require that activities in space be non-aggressive, or in other words, in compliance with the requirements under the United Nations Charter and international law to refrain from the threat or use of force except in accordance with the law, such as in self-defense or pursuant to United Nations Security Council authorization.

✪ ✪ **Non-interference.** Article IX calls on states to enter into international consultations before engaging in activities likely to cause harmful interference with another nation's peaceful uses of outer space.

✪ **Other Space Treaties.** Other major treaties pertaining to space are the 1968 Agreement on the Rescue of Astronauts, the Return of Astronauts and the Return of Objects Launched into Outer Space (The Rescue and Return Agreement), the 1972 Convention on the International Liability for Damage Caused by Space Objects (Liability Convention) and the Convention on Registration of Objects Launched into Outer Space (Registration Convention) of 1974. The Rescue and Return Agreement obligates nations to cooperate in the rescue and return of distressed astronauts and to take those measures it deems practicable to return space objects of other nations that come to Earth within its territory. The Liability Convention provides a system for assessing liability for damage caused by space objects. Generally, a nation is responsible for damage caused by a space object to objects on the ground or to aircraft in flight. Damage caused to other space objects, on the other hand, will only lead to liability if one party can establish fault on the part of the other party. Finally, the Registration Convention requires nations to notify the UN "as soon as practicable" after an object has been launched into outer space, providing certain descriptive information, to include orbital parameters and a general statement of the purpose of the space object.

✪ **Arms Control Treaties.** A few arms control treaties have provisions with some impact on space operations. The Limited Test Ban Treaty, for example, prohibits nuclear explosions in space. Many arms limitations treaties also prohibit interference with "national technical means" of treaty verification. These national technical means include certain surveillance satellites. During times of hostilities, however, arms control treaty obligations may be suspended as between belligerents to the extent those terms are inconsistent with a state of armed conflict.

- **Space Policy.** National and DOD policy have long asserted that the US is committed to exploration and use of outer space by all nations for peaceful purposes and for the benefit of all humanity. US policy has consistently been that peaceful purposes include defense and intelligence purposes. The US further recognizes the right of all nations to engage in the exploration and use of outer space free from harmful interference. In fact, national and DOD space policy state that "[p]urposeful interference with US space systems will be viewed as an infringement on sovereign rights." Finally, both US and DOD policy specifically assign DOD the four space mission areas of space support, space force enhancement, space control, and space force application.

CHAPTER FOUR

EXECUTING SPACE OPERATIONS

 *...[As] we showed and proved during DESERT STORM, and proved again during the air campaign over the Balkans, space is an integral part of everything we do to accomplish our mission. Today, the ultimate high ground is space.*

—General Lester P. Lyles
Commander, Air Force Materiel Command

During force employment, execution of space operations is a dynamic task that requires timely integration throughout the joint campaign. The employment of space forces at the operational level is accomplished through tasking orders that deconflict, synchronize, and integrate space operations with theater operations. Although no authority exists for control over non-military space assets, the joint force must integrate with enabling space operations conducted by non-military space assets. Also, during operations, the adversary will seek to disrupt friendly space capabilities. This asymmetric attack against our space capabilities could threaten our ability to maintain space superiority. Airmen must prepare for an attack of this nature and execute space operations in an integrated manner.

EXECUTION OF GLOBAL FORCES

USSTRATCOM executes a strategy based on requests from multiple theaters, global requirements for national defense, and maintenance of on-orbit space assets. When forces are employed, execution of the space tasking order is a dynamic task requiring timely deconfliction, integration, and synchronization with other elements of the theater campaign. Integrating various space-related or space-based capabilities is accomplished through deliberate coordination processes between the theater AOC and the Space AOC/JSpOC.

Space AOC/JSpOC

The Air Force provides a Space AOC that forms the core of the JSpOC. The Space AOC/JSpOC is located at Vandenberg AFB CA. It includes personnel, facilities and equipment necessary to plan, execute and assess space operations and integrate space power.

The Space AOC/JSpOC tracks assigned and attached space forces/assets and provide reachback support to organic theater space personnel. The Space AOC/JSpOC translates CDRUSSTRATCOM's OPORDs and CDR JFCC Space guidance into the STO. STOs task and direct assigned and attached space forces to fulfill theater and global mission requirements in support of national objectives. The STO cycle is flexible to synchronize with the theater's battle rhythm.

Space AOC/JSpOC Organization

The Space AOC/JSpOC is a functional AOC composed of four divisions: Strategy, combat plans, combat operations, and ISR. There are also specialty teams, liaisons from other agencies and sister Service personnel to enable the Space AOC to fulfill its responsibilities as the JSpOC. Collectively, they accomplish the main processes of strategy development, planning, tasking, collection management and intelligence analysis/production. The Space AOC/JSpOC serves as the focal point for coordination and reachback support for regional space operations requirements. Organized along the structure of an AOC, the Space AOC/JSpOC consists of four divisions that focus on global and theater space operations:

Space AOC/JSpOC is located at Vandenberg AFB CA

☼ **Strategy Division.** The strategy division recommends both long- and short-term strategies to achieve USSTRATCOM and theater objectives by developing, refining, disseminating, and assessing strategy. This is normally presented through the JSOP and space operations directive (SOD), which will be used to guide tasking order development, and during crisis action planning will be expanded or modified to meet the crisis situation. The strategy division is organized into three teams: Strategy development team, strategy guidance team, and operational assessment team.

☼ ☼ **Strategy Development Team** produces the JSOP based on strategic and theater plans, established doctrine, and global space requirements.

☼ ☼ **Strategy Guidance Team** produces the SOD and ensures theater air operations directive and USSTRATCOM OPORDs and FRAGOs are linked to the overall objectives.

☼ ☼ **Operational Assessment Team** collects information provided by combat operations and other sources and performs an operational assessment of the space effects being generated. The operational assessment team analyzes the effectiveness of previous STO executions which may guide future strategy development.

Each of these teams has individuals who are matrixed from other Space AOC/JSpOC divisions to provide subject area expertise for development of strategy division products.

❂ **Combat Plans Division.** The combat plans division performs operational planning to develop execution orders for joint space operations. The combat plans division publishes and disseminates the STO. This document applies specific space capabilities and assets to accomplish tasks in fulfillment of global USSTRATCOM and/or theater missions. The combat plans division is divided into two teams, the master space plan team and STO production team.

  ❂ ❂ **Master Space Plan Team** defines space effects and builds the master space plan (MSP). The MSP is similar to the master air attack plan.

  ❂ ❂ **STO Production Team** uses the MSP to produce an executable STO. Accompanying SPINs are also included in the STO.

  The STO production cycle is based on the six-step targeting cycle described in joint doctrine. The cycle is typically designed around the joint standard of 72 hours (48 hours for planning and 24 hours for execution). However, the cycle is flexible to synchronize with the warfighter's battle rhythm requirements.

❂ **Combat Operations Division (COD).** The COD monitors execution of the current tasking order and publishes any required changes. The COD maintains space situational awareness and provides a 24/7 reachback interface for theater AOCs. Timely coordination between the COD and each tasked wing operations center (WOC) is essential for effective tasking order execution. Wing commanders and their squadrons receive orders, directives, and other guidance from the Space AOC/JSpOC through the WOC.

  The Space AOC/JSpOC has aligned itself according to functions based on effects based approach to operations. These concepts describe the capabilities and effects space forces contribute to the joint fight. They include space superiority; global information services; global surveillance, tracking and targeting; assured access; space force application; and space C2.

  ❂ ❂ **Space Superiority** is that level of control in the space domain that one force enjoys over another that permits the conduct of operations at a given time and place without prohibitive interference by the opposing force. Space superiority may be localized in time and space, or it may be broad and persistent. Achieving space superiority is of primary concern since it allows control and exploitation of the space domain in order to provide space effects in and through space. The Air Force achieves space superiority through counterspace operations, including offensive and defensive operations, both of which are based on robust space situational awareness.

  For more detailed discussion of space superiority, refer to AFDD 2-2.1, *Counterspace Operations.*

  ❂ ❂ **Global Information Services**. One of the primary effects space assets provide is the transmission and distribution of information. Global information services describes space assets ability to contribute to information superiority and includes such capabilities as positioning, navigation, and timing; satellite communications; and blue force tracking.

- ✪ ✪ **Global Surveillance, Tracking and Targeting** describes abilities of space assets to conduct surveillance and reconnaissance, enabling other functions like weather and missile warning.

- ✪ ✪ **Assured Access.** Our capabilities to gain access and operate in the space domain describe assured access to space. This includes launch and range operations, satellite control networks, as well as terrestrial communication networks that link ground nodes of our C2 systems.

- ✪ ✪ **Space Force Applications** are those forces that deliver kinetic effects to, from, or through space. While only ICBM systems currently fall into this category, future space systems, such as the common aerospace vehicle, land-based strategic deterrent, and conventional ICBM, could deliver combat effects to terrestrial and space targets.

- ✪ ✪ **C2 of Space Forces.** C2 provides the ability to monitor, assess, plan, and execute space forces in an integrated and comprehensive manner.

- ✪ **ISR Division.** The ISR Division (ISRD) is focused on providing the strategic, operational, tactical, and technical knowledge about adversary capabilities necessary to effectively plan US operations. Since knowledge of adversary capabilities, tactics, strengths, and weaknesses is necessary to optimally plan and execute both offensive and defensive operations, ISRD personnel support all Space AOC/JSpOC divisions. ISRD activities include IPOE, maintaining adversary orders of battle, enemy COA prediction, identifying and tracking critical indicators of pending foreign activity, recognizing and predicting foreign patterns and behavior, and providing target system analysis and target nomination lists.

Integrating Global with Theater Space Operations

To ensure theater military space requirements are met, appropriate command relationships should be established. Control of military space forces is normally retained by USSTRATCOM due to the global nature of space assets. Support is the normal command relationship used to integrate USSTRATCOM space operations and theater operations. These command relationships allow theaters to coordinate with the supporting commander to integrate space capabilities. **An established relationship between the CFACC and the CDR JFCC Space is essential to ensure flexibility and responsiveness when integrating space operations.** Additionally, DIRLAUTH should be authorized for coordinated planning.

The Space AOC/JSpOC normally synchronizes its supporting operations with the theaters because the supported commander drives tasking requirements. By adjusting its operational schedule, the Space AOC/JSpOC optimizes support to the theater and space integration. If more than one theater is being supported, an operational schedule will be adjusted to balance support to all theaters.

Examples of Global Space Forces In Support Of Theater Operations

Operation DESERT STORM, Missile Warning – Prior to DESERT STORM, the DSP had been used to support missile warning for ICBM launches against North America. During DESERT STORM, command relationships were established between US Space Command (the predecessor to USSTRATCOM) and US Central Command so that US Space Command provided missile warning to the theater via military satellite communications. During the operation, DSP detected 87 SCUD launches. A warning sent to the theater allowed time for the Saudis, US forces, and the allied forces to seek shelter from incoming SCUDs. The data was also used for attack operations (SCUD hunting) and Patriot operations (SCUD in-flight destruction). Based on the lessons learned from DESERT STORM, new space units were created to improve warning operations to the theater, such as the 11 SWS.

Operation ALLIED FORCE, Munitions Guidance – Munitions using GPS for guidance became a requirement for what Admiral James Ellis (Commander of Allied Forces Southern Europe; and former Commander, JTF Noble Anvil) called 'A War of Weather.' Precision-guided munitions were no longer "good enough." In this operation, pilots experienced a greater than 50 percent cloud cover more than 70 percent of the time. Laser and electro-optical-guided munitions simply could not hit what the pilots could not see. GPS-aided munitions allowed allied forces to operate at night and in poor weather conditions eliminating enemy sanctuaries and operational lulls.

Operation ALLIED FORCE, Battle Damage Indications (BDI) – Through a direct support relationship between the 11 SWS (CONUS) and the CFACC (Italy), real-time information from DSP was fed to the CAOC. This information, coupled with data from unmanned aircraft (UA) and imaging satellites provided BDI to tailor follow-on strike packages. This increased situational awareness for analysts and operators.

Operation IRAQI FREEDOM, All-weather employment and Defensive Counterspace Operations – GPS guidance and navigation continued to be critical to joint operations. During a sandstorm, the Air Force was able to continue to strike enemy ground forces in close contact with friendly forces, effectively denying the adversary an operational sanctuary. OIF also provided the first operational experience showing the vulnerability of the GPS signal to electronic attack when Iraqi forces attempted to jam GPS. Ironically, some of the GPS jammers were destroyed with GPS-aided munitions, the first real-world example of the counterspace mission called suppression of adversary counterspace capabilities.

EXECUTION OF SPACE FORCES IN THEATER

Today, there are multi-Service space forces that can deploy to support operations. Some of these forces are designed to integrate into various levels of command within the joint force. Other deployable space forces possess capabilities that must be integrated into the overall military campaign. Depending on theater requirements and the global situation, the SecDef may attach these forces to geographic combatant commanders conducting combat operations.

When deployed, Air Force space forces are normally attached to an AETF under the OPCON of the COMAFFOR. When the COMAFFOR is dual-hatted as the CFACC, the CFACC is normally given TACON of other Service space forces in excess of their organic requirements. The CFACC should integrate and task assigned, attached, and other Service forces into operations via the AOC and the ATO process. Air Force space experts are matrixed across the AOC, ensuring space capabilities and effects are integrated into theater operations via the ATO, for deployed space forces, and STO, for global space forces.

Examples of Theater Space Forces in Operations

Vietnam War – Even though USSTRATCOM and AFSPC were decades from formation, a significant example of deployed space forces occurred during the Vietnam War. Two DMSP ground stations were deployed to theater. One went to Vietnam and the other went to Thailand to support military operations with weather data. Weather was a major concern during Vietnam. The DMSP satellites became the primary short-term forecasting tool for tactical military operations. The impact was profound. The commander of Air Force operations in Southeast Asia stated: "As far as I am concerned, this [satellite] weather picture is probably the greatest innovation of the war."

Air Force Space Support Teams (AFSSTs) (1993-2000) – The AFSSTs deployed to several operations, supporting the JFACC in the AOC by providing space education and expertise. Due to the success of the AFSST, the Air Force recognized the need to integrate space expertise into theater staffs. By the end of 2000, the Air Force had deactivated the AFSSTs and begun the integration of space forces across the combat air forces.

Korea – Currently, the air component commander uses a deployable data downlink station operated by the Army and Navy to integrate an in-theater capability to support theater missile warning operations. The JTAGS provides data for warning and attack operations against ballistic missile attack. The Air Force provides mission data to JTAGS via the DSP satellite.

INTEGRATING CIVIL, COMMERCIAL, FOREIGN SPACE ASSETS

Today, many civil, commercial, and foreign organizations contribute space capabilities to military operations. Some organizations, such as those within the communications and intelligence communities, have established processes for military forces to request services. Non-military space assets provide alternatives to meet the military's operational needs.

Military resources will be stressed during large-scale contingencies and combat operations. In these situations, the military normally will use civil, commercial, and/or foreign space assets to support military objectives. The integration of non-military space assets may become vital to mission accomplishment. Military capabilities may be augmented with these assets or the assets may, by themselves, meet the military's needs. In most cases, the geographic combatant commander's staff will determine the appropriate avenue for meeting warfighter needs using these assets.

Civil, commercial, and foreign space assets can be leveraged through pre-established agreements, but often must be requested on an unplanned basis. For example, the military may request NASA to redirect focus from a scientific mission to support a military operation. DOD organizations like the National Geospatial-Intelligence Agency and Defense Information Systems Agency are designated to contract with commercial entities for services. In any case, because of unique C2 processes, pre-established agreements enhance effectiveness.

National and civil organizations are responsive to warfighter requirements in most instances. There may be instances, however, where competing requirements must be balanced, such as strategic reconnaissance for treaty verification that compete with operational collection requirements. Also, when dealing with commercial entities, military commanders may not expect the same level of support as with DOD or civil agencies. Corporations are market driven and concerned with their long-term success. There may be situations where commercial entities conclude it is not in their best interest to support certain military operations.

Similarly, foreign space assets, even those provided by our allies, may not be easily integrated into military operations. Civil, commercial, and/or foreign space assets may be specialized and not have sufficient flexibility for dynamic re-tasking, may require unique procedures and equipment, and may not meet critical requirements for military operations.

Examples Of Civil/Commercial Space Assets In The Fight

Vietnam War – During the Vietnam War, the military used a NASA communications satellite, the synchronous communications satellite, to provide communications between Saigon and Hawaii. Also, the military leased commercial satellite communications circuits to connect Saigon and Hawaii to meet administrative and logistical needs. Satellite usage during the Vietnam conflict established the military practice of relying on civil and commercial space systems.

Operation DESERT STORM – Civil remote sensing satellites played a key role in providing wide-area information in the theater. The Pentagon spent up to $6M on data from the US-owned Land Remote Sensing Satellite and French-owned SPOT imaging satellites. These satellites were used to provide wide-area surveillance to augment and complement US intelligence satellites.

Operation ALLIED FORCE – During the later stages of the campaign, 60 percent of satellite communications was provided by commercial entities. This is a significant change from DESERT STORM where only 15 percent of communications was provided by commercial satellites.

Operation ATLAS RESPONSE – An Air Force-led JTF was deployed in March 2000 to Mozambique and South Africa to conduct humanitarian assistance/disaster relief for flooding in the region. During initial deployment and setup, the JTF staff found overhead imagery from a NASA experimental satellite posted on the NASA web site. The images showed the difference in saturation of the land following the flooding. The JTF had no formal relationship with NASA, but used the images to build situational awareness on the region.

Operation IRAQI FREEDOM – During OIF, military satellite communications did not meet the significant bandwidth requirements of the joint force during major combat operations. Consequently, the military contracted commercial satellite communications to supply nearly 80% of communications during the operation. As requirements for increased communications bandwidth continue to rise, the US military will continue to seek commercial satellite alternatives to augment our capabilities.

RESPONDING TO AN ASYMMETRIC ATTACK AGAINST US SPACE CAPABILITIES

The US is the most advanced space power in world. The US is also the most space-dependent country in the world. Today, most adversaries will not be able to directly overcome the US or its allies' dominance in space, which makes an asymmetric attack against friendly space capabilities attractive. For example, some adversaries have a limited ability to attack links or nodes of our space systems. During Operation IRAQI FREEDOM, the adversary employed GPS jammers to interfere with coalition weapons employment. Military planners and operators must be prepared for electronic as well as other types of attacks.

Decision makers in the AOC must understand that time-sensitive requirements necessitate a responsive relationship with reachback agencies who can anticipate possible situations and to react quickly. Normally, when establishing the command relationship, the supported/supporting commanders discuss how to handle time-sensitive situations. Command relationships need to be flexible enough to support time-sensitive operations. Because of the impacts of asymmetric attacks against space capabilities, theater and Space AOCs need to discuss time-sensitive processes early in planning process.

Asymmetric attacks may be in violation of various international laws and agreements. Depending on the nature of the attack, interagency and international cooperation may play a significant role in responding to such attacks. In a given circumstance, the sequenced or simultaneous employment of the diplomatic, informational and economic instruments of national power may complement or even obviate the need for a military response.

CHAPTER FIVE

DEVELOPMENT OF SPACE PROFESSIONALS

... the US must, over the next few years, develop a cadre of experienced, intensely knowledgeable people skilled in applying space to combat. We are talking about an entirely new breed of war fighters, who will ultimately transform the power and scope of warfighting in the same way airpower professionals have done in the last century.

—The Honorable Peter B. Teets
Former Acting Secretary of the Air Force,
Director of the National Reconnaissance Office,
and DOD Executive Agent for Space

Developing Airmen is an Air Force core competency, and the development of a space professional cadre is recognized as an enabling capability for employing integrated space capabilities that support the full spectrum of military operations. Space professional training and education instill space-mindedness, make space capabilities universally understood, accepted, and exploitable by joint forces, and create military and civilian space leaders with a stronger foundation in space employment and a greater understanding of space capabilities.

SPACE TRAINING AND EVALUATION

Space operators should be trained throughout their careers to integrate space across the range of military operations and during all phases of an operation. Continual training is crucial to maintain proficiency because space assets and their TTPs continually evolve. In concert with training, evaluation is key to identifying shortfalls and is a critical measure of training program effectiveness. Stringent standards of performance should be established to ensure space operators attain and maintain the high degree of proficiency required for mission success. Commanders at all levels should be involved with the training and evaluation of their personnel and should be confident they meet minimum standards before being certified mission ready.

Following training common to all space professionals, space operators initially become specialists in a specific area or system. However, the diverse nature of space operations dictates that, over time, they should gain knowledge and understanding of the broad spectrum of space operations. As their careers progress, space operators should move beyond technical knowledge of their core specialty areas and gain a more operational-level focus of air and space power. Ultimately, the Air Force needs Airmen who are space professionals and can articulate how space operations integrate into, contribute to, and improve military operations.

EXERCISES

Exercises are conducted to achieve training objectives. For training to best prepare participants for actual requirements, exercises should be planned and conducted to resemble real operations as closely as possible. Space forces are no exception and should be realistically exercised to the full extent possible, consistent with operational requirements. To improve readiness, space forces should participate as a full partner with air and information assets in large-scale exercises overseas and in the US. Joint exercises in overseas locations provide realistic training for in-theater and deployable Air Force forces, and also allow other Services and allied military forces to gain valuable experience in integrating space capabilities. When it is impossible to meet mission requirements and take part in an exercise, high fidelity simulators should be used to present the correct "space picture" to participants.

Integrated Air, Space, and Information Test Range

There are several ranges and exercises that prepare Air Force forces for joint operations. As new space capabilities are developed, test ranges such as the space test and training range evaluate new capabilities prior to operational fielding. The development of an integrated test range for air, space, and information assets enables the Air Force to conduct enhanced testing, training, and exercises against potential adversary space force capabilities. It also integrates Air Force forces in an operational environment prior to real-world contingency operations. This training enhances the Air Force's ability to effectively integrate capabilities and produce the commander's desired effects.

EDUCATION

Education broadens understanding of space's overall contribution to military operations and gives operators an appreciation of how their specific area of expertise impacts global and theater operations. Education is necessary to move space professionals beyond the tactical and technical focus of their day-to-day jobs and to assure the requisite level of technological skills necessary to sustain the space mission. Space education goes beyond individual service requirements and encompasses all organizations within the national security space environment.

Developmental Education (DE)

DE provides broad education appropriate for different points in an Airman's career as a space professional. These programs provide a perspective on the role of space power in military operations through study of such subjects as Air Force and joint doctrine. An understanding of these areas is critical for Airmen to effectively employ space power within a joint and coalition environment. DE also provides the opportunity for all Airmen to learn about the application of space in military operations.

WARGAMES

Wargames are used for educating personnel and testing of new concepts of employment and organization. Because the United States has yet to meet a "space peer" in conflict, wargames continue to be a primary means of assessing the potential doctrinal implications of the use of space systems. Wargames generate insights into the current and future uses of space in warfighting. This venue allows the US to test potential actions used by adversaries to attack our space capabilities. An important element in wargames is to demonstrate unanticipated consequences involved with future space capabilities including vulnerabilities, policy, and force structure concerns. Space forces should be modeled in a realistic fashion consistent with other military forces.

RED TEAMING

Red Teaming provides a capability to conduct vulnerability assessments used to prepare combat air forces, joint and allied forces for combat by providing challenging, realistic space threat replication, training, and feedback. Experiencing the tactics and capabilities adversaries may use against us will help ensure we maintain the space superiority we need to prevail in real world scenarios.

EXPERIMENTS

Experiments are used for evaluating operational concepts and new technologies. Through experiments, the Air Force gains knowledge about future systems technology and processes, spiral development of developing technology and processes, and rapid transition of proven technology and processes to the warfighter. Experimentation is fundamentally different from exercises. Exercises involve training all personnel in established processes on fielded systems. Combatant commanders are encouraged to conduct experiments to test new operating concepts. However, because experiments are designed to be repeated, desired system and process knowledge is gained. However, lessons learned should not be overstated given the carefully orchestrated nature of experiments.

SUGGESTED READINGS

Air Force Publications (Note: All Air Force doctrine documents are available on the Air Force Doctrine Center web page at https://www.doctrine.af.mil)

Air Force Doctrine Document 1, *Air Force Basic Doctrine*
Air Force Doctrine Document 2, *Operations and Organization*
Air Force Doctrine Document 2-2.1, *Counterspace Operations*
Air Force Operational Tactics, Techniques, and Procedures 2-3.4, *Joint Space Operations Center*
Air Force Tactics, Techniques, and Procedures 3-1.28, *Space*

Joint Publications

Joint Publication 0-2, *Unified Action Armed Forces (UNAAF)*
Joint Publication 3-0, *Joint Operations*
Joint Publication 3-14, *Joint Doctrine for Space Operations*
Joint Publication 3-30, *Command and Control for Joint Air Operations*

Other Publications

Arnold, David C., *Spying from Space: Constructing America's Satellite Command and Control Networks* (College Station: Texas A&M University Press, 2005).

Air University Space Primer, (Air University Press), Aug 2003

Cleary, Mark C., *The Cape: Military Space Operations, 1971–1992* (45th Space Wing, History Office), 1994.

Gorn, Michael H., *Harnessing the Genie, Science and Technology Forecasting for the Air Force 1944-1986* (Office of Air Force History), 1988.

Goure, Daniel, and Christopher M. Szara, *Air and Space Power in the New Millennium* (Center for Strategic and International Studies), 1997.

Hayes, Peter, *Space Power for the Next Millenium* (Air University Press), 2000.

Jelonek, Mark P., *Toward an Air and Space Force: Naval Aviation and the Implications for Space Power* (Air University Press), 1999.

Johnson-Freese, Joan, and Roger Handberg, *Space, the Dormant Frontier: Changing the Paradigm for the 21st Century* (Praeger), 1997.

Lupton, David, *On Space Warfare* (Air University Press), 1988.

MacDougall, Walter A., *...the Heavens and the Earth* (Johns Hopkins University Press), 1985.

Mantz, Michael R., *The New Sword: A Theory of Space Combat Power* (Air University Press), 1995.

Oberg, James, *Space Power Theory*, GPO, 1999.

Peebles, Curtis, High Frontier: *The U.S. Air Force and the Military Space Program* (Air Force History and Museums Program), 1997.

Preston, Bob, *Plowshares and Power: The Military Use of Civil Space* (National Defense University Press), 1994.

Report of the Commission to Assess United States National Security Space Management and Organization, 2001.

Spires, David N., *Beyond Horizons: A Half Century of Air Force Space Leadership* (Air Force Space Command), 1997.

United Nations, United Nations Treaties and Principles on Outer Space: text and status of treaties and principles governing the activities of states in the exploration and use of outer space, adopted by the United Nations General Assembly (Office for Outer Space Affairs, United Nations), 1994.

US Army Field Manual 3-14, *Space Support to Army Operations.*

APPENDIX A

ORBITAL FUNDAMENTALS

1. Strengths and Limitations of Space Operations

Because the constellation design and orbital characteristics of a space system can vary greatly, space operations' strengths and limitations must be considered. In general, space systems provide the ultimate high ground without overflight restrictions. The absence of significant drag and other natural opposing forces also allows space systems to have increased longevity, sometimes limited only by the reliability of the systems themselves (see Figure A.1). However, there are several forces at work that slowly degrade the accuracy of a satellite's location: atmospheric drag (air particles and atoms exist even at very high altitudes); gravitational attractions of the sun, moon, and other planets; the fact that the Earth is not a perfect sphere and the force of gravity varies; gentle pressure from solar radiation; and the interaction of solar radiation and the Earth's geomagnetic environment.

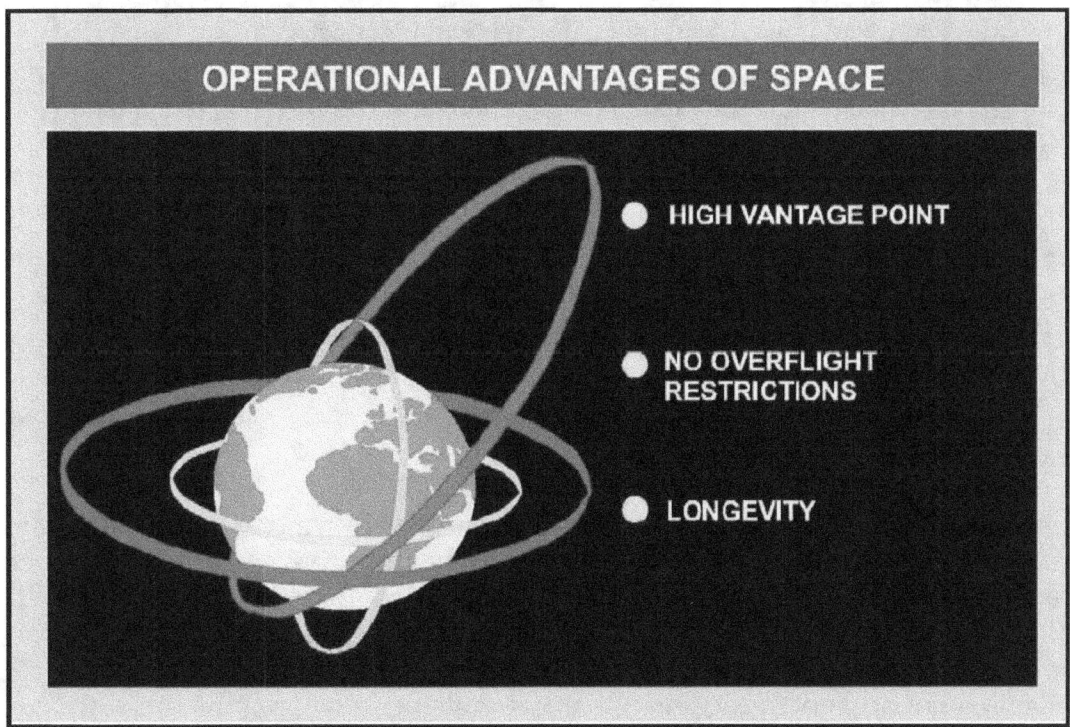

Figure A.1. Operational Advantages of Space.

2. A Satellite Orbital Period

The size of a satellite's orbit determines its period, or the time it takes to complete one revolution. The lower the orbital altitude, the shorter the period. Common orbits have periods ranging from about 90 minutes (low orbits just above the atmosphere) to 24 hours ("geosynchronous" orbits approximately 22,300 statute miles above the Earth's surface) (see Figure A.2).

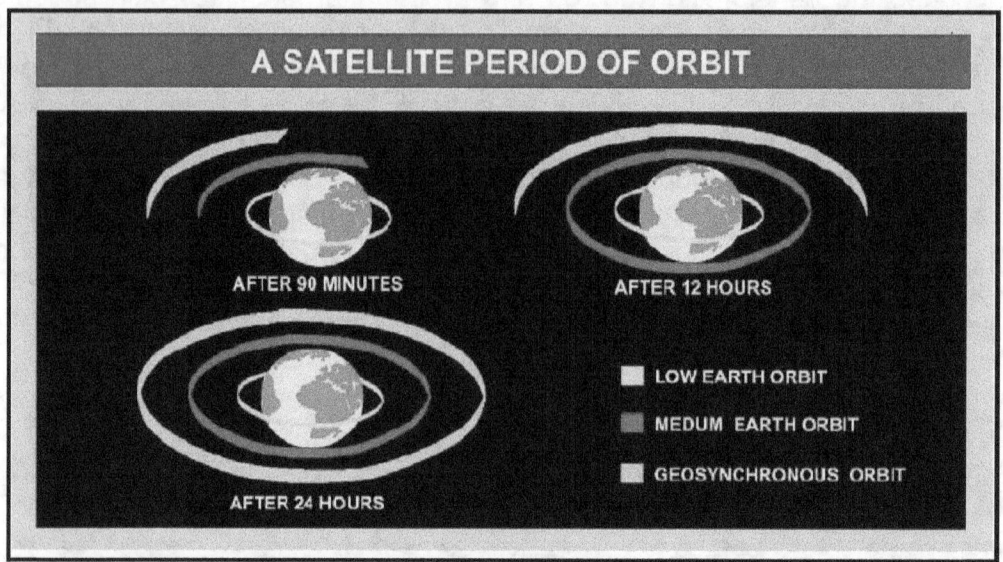

Figure A.2. A Satellite Orbital Period.

3. Eccentricity

Eccentricity is used to describe how much an orbit's shape deviates from a circle. The figure ranges from 0 to 1 with a value of 0 for a circular orbit.

4. Inclination

A satellite's inclination is the angle between the Earth's equatorial plane and the satellite's orbital plane (measured counterclockwise from the equatorial to the orbital plane at the point where the satellite's path crosses the equator headed northward) (see Figure A.3). This angle determines what part of the Earth's surface passes directly beneath the satellite—a critical consideration in accomplishing its mission (see Figure A.4). Depending on the inclination, a single satellite may not be able to provide coverage of a specific point on or region of the Earth. However, a constellation may have that capability. Other space assets—civil, commercial, international, and military—may be used to supplement the satellite's capability and provide continuous, non-intrusive coverage.

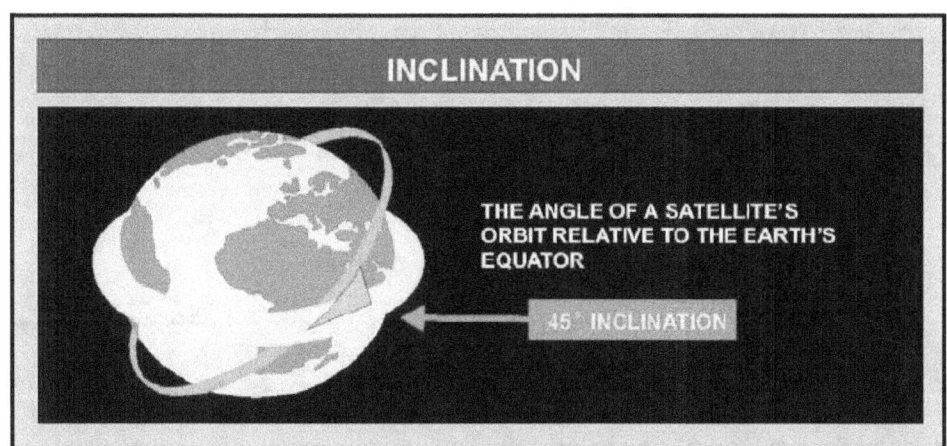

Figure A.3. Inclination .

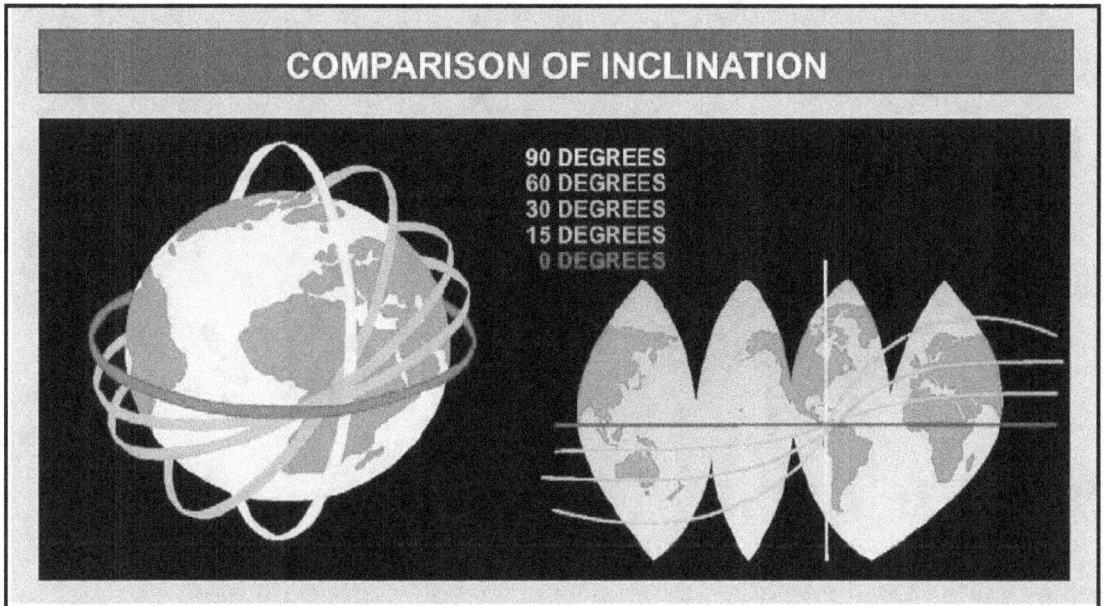

Figure A.4. Comparison of Inclination.

5. Types of Orbits (See Figure A.5)

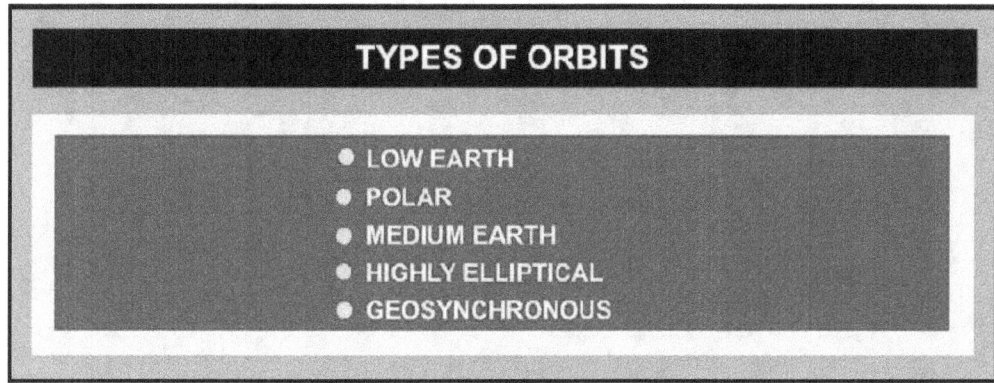

Figure A.5. Types of Orbits.

a. Low Earth Orbit (LEO). LEO is the easiest type of orbit to reach, and the satellite's proximity to the Earth's surface provides the best potential for high-resolution imagery (see Figure A.6). However, satellites in these orbits can view a smaller portion of the surface of the Earth at any one time than those at higher altitudes, and atmospheric drag can shorten mission duration. LEO applications include manned flight, environmental monitoring and other ISR, and communication missions.

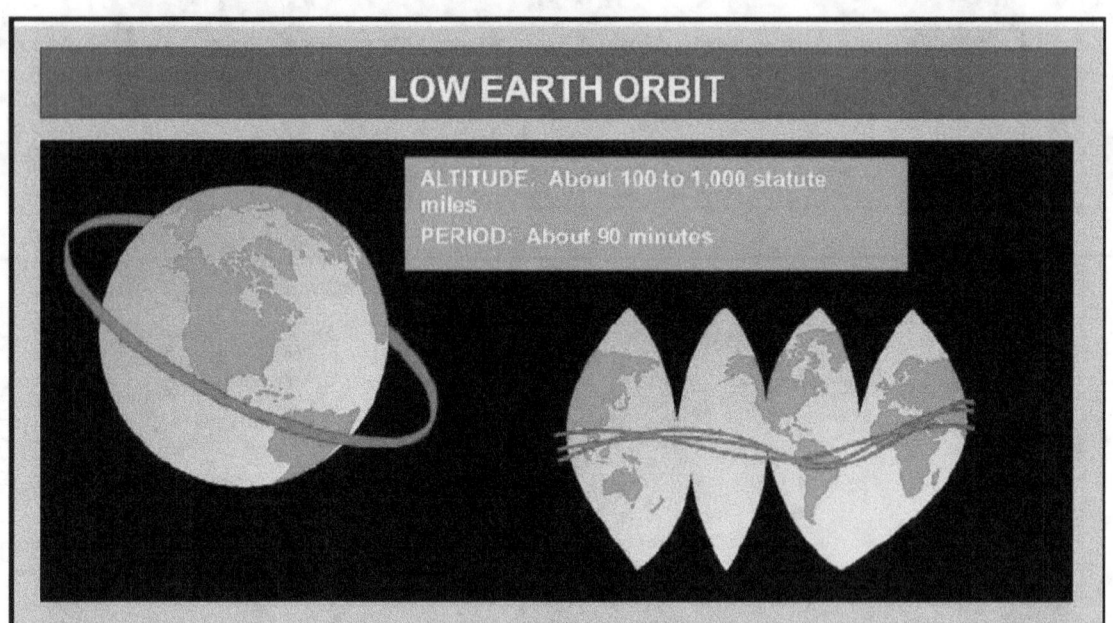

Figure A.6. Low Earth Orbit .

b. Polar Orbits. A polar orbit is one with an inclination near 90 degrees. A satellite in a polar orbit will travel pole to pole, covering all or almost all of the surface of the earth in 12 to 24 hours, making this type of orbit very useful for environmental monitoring and other ISR missions. A particular type of near polar orbit is a sun synchronous orbit. It has an inclination of 90 to 120 degrees and maintains a constant orientation towards the sun throughout the year, resulting in similar lighting conditions every orbit and making it very useful to detect changes in environmental conditions or surface features of the Earth over time.

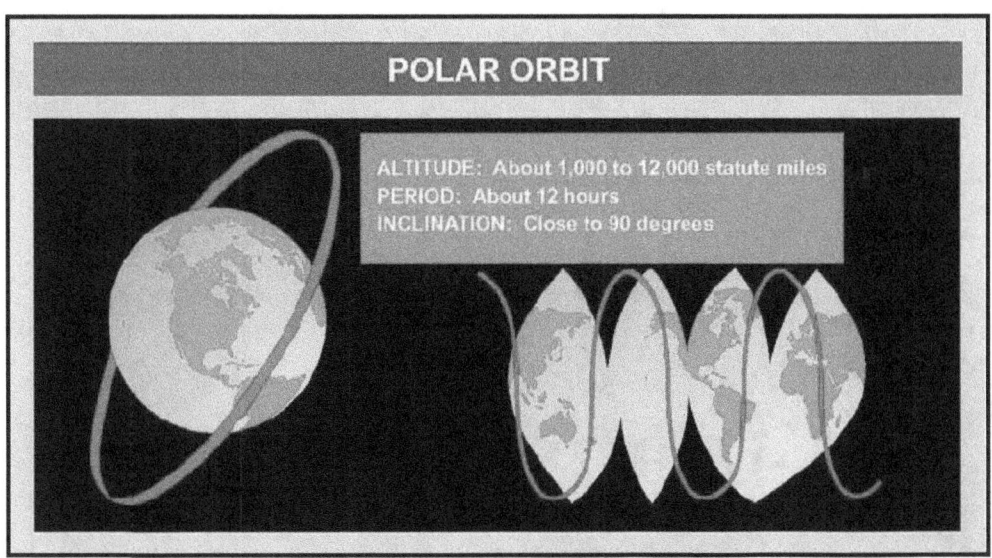

Figure A.7. Polar Orbit.

c. Medium Earth Orbit (MEO). MEO provides a satellite a view of a larger portion of the Earth at any one time than LEO. While atmospheric drag is negligible, a lot more energy is required to place a satellite in these orbits (see Figure A.8). Current applications include navigation systems (e.g., GPS).

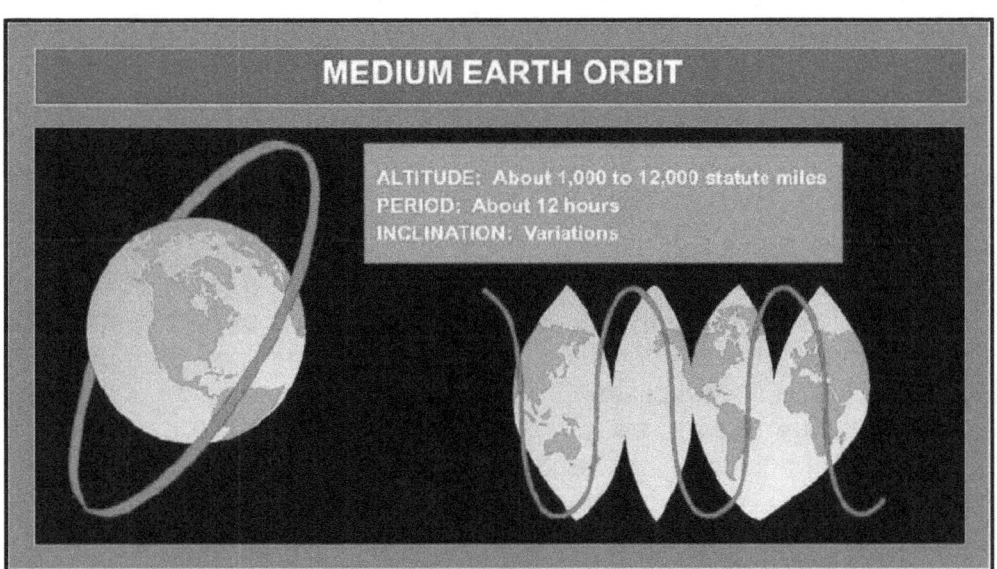

Figure A.8. Medium Earth Orbit .

d. Highly Elliptical Orbit (HEO). HEO is an orbit with a large eccentricity, and an orbit shape of an ellipse vs. a circle. A useful feature of a satellite in a HEO is that the satellite travels relatively slowly when near apogee, giving a long dwell time combined with visibility of a large portion of the Earth. The former Soviet Union made extensive use of a HEO called a Molniya orbit that has a period of 12 hours, an inclination of 63.4 degrees, an eccentricity of 0.7, and an apogee over the Northern Hemisphere (See

Figure A.9). This particular HEO is very useful for providing communications or coverage in the high northern latitudes, a region less well covered by satellites in geostationary orbits. HEO orbits are useful for communications and some ISR missions.

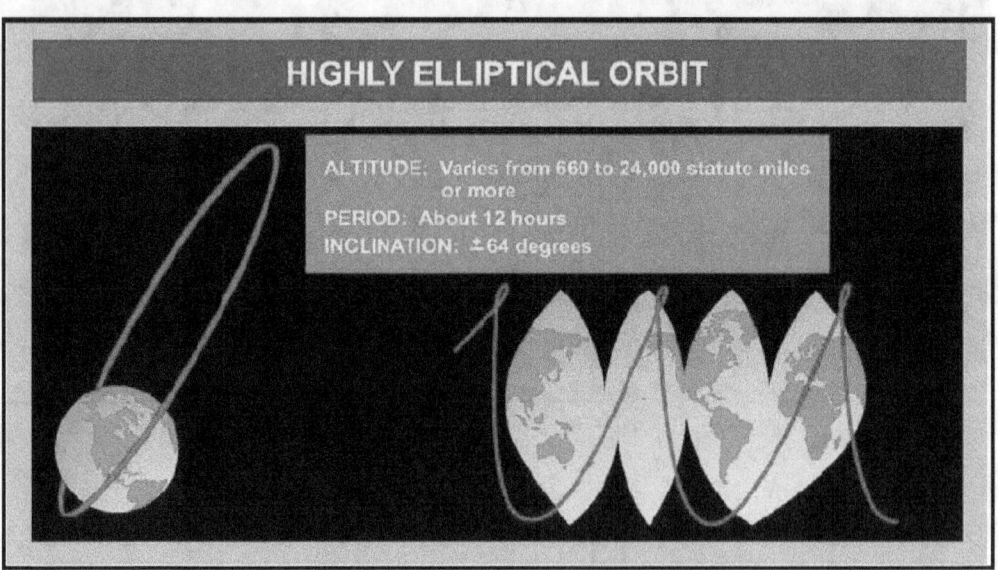

Figure A.9. Highly Elliptical Orbit.

e. Geosynchronous Earth Orbit (GEO). Geostationary satellites are in a near-circular, near-zero inclination orbit with periods exactly equal to the Earth's rotation of 24 hours (see Figure A.10). Hence, geostationary satellites remain roughly over one spot on the Earth at all times. Orbits that have a 24-hour period, but do not have a near-zero inclination or eccentricity, are called geosynchronous. All geostationary satellites are geosynchronous, but not all geosynchronous satellites are geostationary. The ground trace of a GEO satellite looks like a figure "8" pattern when traced onto a Mercator map of the Earth, which reflects the natural oscillations of the orbit as well as the degree to which the orbit is inclined to the Earth's equatorial plane. GEO orbits have an altitude of approximately 22,300 statute miles, are difficult to reach, and require launch vehicles with significant lift capability. Satellites in GEO orbit provide coverage of large areas of the surface of the globe with continuous visibility of these areas. Therefore they are very useful for persistent communications, weather monitoring, and certain ISR functions.

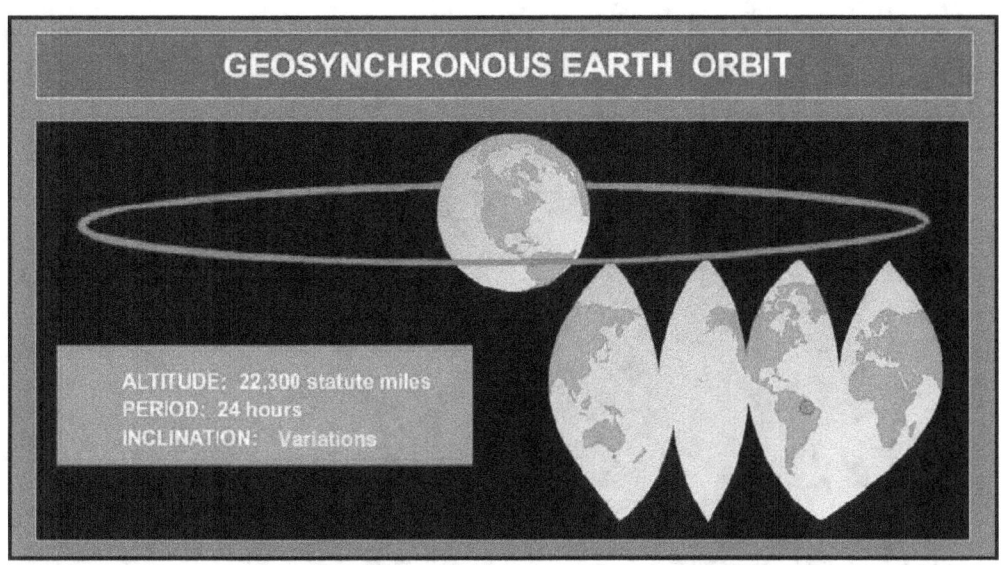

Figure A.10. Geosynchronous Earth Orbit.

6. Constellations

a. When a single satellite cannot provide the coverage necessary to accomplish a given mission, multiple satellites performing a single mission (a constellation) are used to provide global coverage or increase timeliness of coverage (see Figure A.11 and Figure A.12). Navigation constellations (such as GPS) are designed to ensure that signals from multiple satellites can be simultaneously received at a location on the ground, improving the accuracy of the information coming from those satellites. Communications constellations, on the other hand, are designed to ensure that at least one satellite is within line of sight of both ends of the communications link, and may include both equatorial and polar components. ISR constellations have satellites in both high and low altitude orbits, providing both wide-area coverage and high-resolution data.

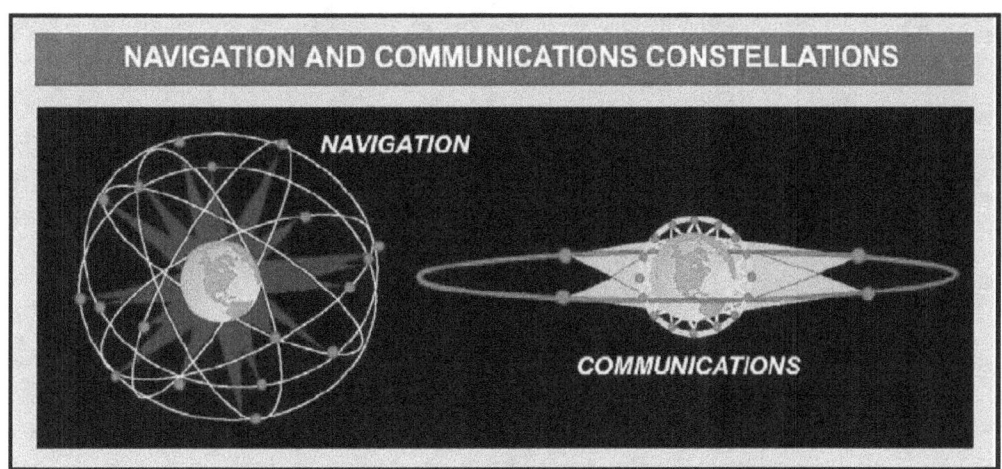

Figure A.11. Typical Constellations.

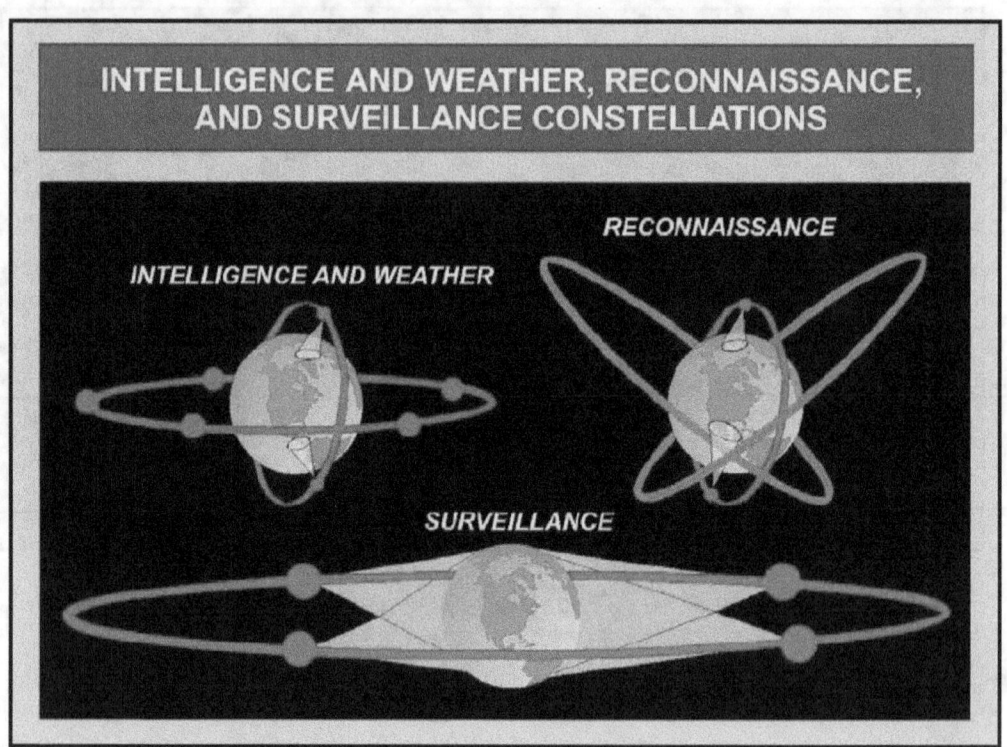

Figure A.12. Intelligence and Weather, Reconnaissance, and Surveillance Constellations.

b. Weather and reconnaissance systems may require constellations that combine high and low altitude systems. This provides on-board sensors with the capability to acquire wide-area, low-resolution coverage and limited field of view, high-resolution coverage, respectively. Some ISR systems, on the other hand, need continuous access to the areas surveyed and usually rely on high altitude, long dwell time orbits.

This appendix is based on information in JP 3-14, *Space Operations*.

GLOSSARY

Abbreviations and Acronyms

AADC	area air defense commander
ACCE	air component coordination element
AETF	air and space expeditionary task force
AFDD	Air Force doctrine document
AFSPC	Air Force Space Command
AFSST	Air Force space support team
AFSPC/CC	Commander, Air Force Space Command
AO	area of operations
AOC	air and space operations center
AOR	area of responsibility
ARABSAT	Arabian Satellite Communications Organization
ATO	air tasking order
BDI	battle damage indications
C2	command and control
CAOC	combined air and space operations center
CAP	crisis action planning
CCDR	combatant commander
CDR	commander
CDRUSSTRATCOM	Commander, United States Strategic Command
CFACC	combined forces air component commander
CFE	commercial and foreign entities
COA	course of action
COD	combat operations division
COCOM	combatant command (command authority)
COMAFFOR	commander, Air Force forces
CONUS	continental United States
DE	developmental education
DIRLAUTH	direct liaison authorized
DIRSPACEFOR	director of space forces
DMSP	Defense Meteorological Satellite Program
DOD	Department of Defense
DSP	Defense Support Program
EBAO	effects-based approach to operations
FRAGO	fragmentary order
GCC	geographic combatant commander

51

GEO	geosynchronous earth orbit
GPS	Global Positioning System
GWOT	global war on terrorism
HEO	highly elliptical orbit
ICBM	intercontinental ballistic missile
INMARSAT	international maritime satellite
INTELSAT	International Telecommunications Satellite Organization
IPOE	intelligence preparation of the operational environment
ISR	intelligence, surveillance, and reconnaissance
ISRD	Intelligence, surveillance, and reconnaissance division
JAOC	joint air and space operations center
JAOP	joint air operations plan
JFACC	joint force air and space component commander
JFC	joint force commander
JFCC	joint functional component command
JOA	joint operations area
JP	joint publication
JSOP	joint space operations plan
JSpOC	Joint Space Operations Center
JTAGS	joint tactical ground station
JTF	joint task force
LEO	low Earth orbit
MEO	medium earth orbit
MSP	master space plan
NASA	National Aeronautics and Space Administration
NOAA	National Oceanic and Atmospheric Administration
OAF	Operation ALLIED FORCE
OIF	Operation IRAQI FREEDOM
OPCON	operational control
OPLAN	operation plan
OPORD	operation order
OST	Outer Space Treaty
PNT	Positioning, navigation, and timing
POTUS	President of the United States
ROE	rules of engagement
SBIRS	Space-based Infrared System

SC	space control
SCA	space coordinating authority
SecDef	Secretary of Defense
SFA	space force application
SFE	space force enhancement
SOD	space operations directive
SOPS	space operations squadron
SPINS	special instructions
SS	space support
STO	space tasking order
SWS	space warning squadron
TACON	tactical control
TTP	tactics, techniques, and procedures
UA	unmanned aircraft
USSTRATCOM	United States Strategic Command
WOC	wing operations center

Definitions

coordinating authority. A commander or individual assigned responsibility for coordinating specific functions or activities involving forces of two or more Military Departments or two or more forces of the same Service. The commander or individual has the authority to require consultation between agencies involved, but does not have the authority to compel agreement. In the event that essential agreement cannot be obtained, the matter shall be referred to the appointing authority. Coordinating authority is a consultation relationship, not an authority through which command may be exercised. Coordinating authority is more applicable to planning and similar activities than to operations. (JP 1-02)

direction. Guidance to or management of support staff functions. Inherent within command but not a command authority in its own right. In some cases, can be considered an explicit instruction or order. Used by commanders and their designated subordinates to facilitate, channel, or motivate support staff to achieve appropriate action, tempo, or intensity. Used by directors of staff agencies on behalf of the commander to provide guidance to their staffs on how best to accomplish stated objectives IAW the commander's intent. (AFDD 1)

joint force air component commander. The commander within a unified command, subordinate unified command, or joint task force responsible to the establishing commander for making recommendations on the proper employment of assigned, attached, and/or made available for tasking air forces; planning and coordinating air operations; or accomplishing such operational missions as may be assigned. The joint force air component commander is given the authority necessary to accomplish missions and tasks assigned by the establishing commander. Also called **JFACC**. See also joint force commander. (JP 1-02) [*The joint force air and space component commander (JFACC) uses the joint air and space operations center to command and control the integrated air and space effort to meet the joint force commander's objectives. This title emphasizes the US Air Force position that air power and space power together create effects that cannot be achieved through air or space power alone.*] [AFDD 2] {Words in brackets apply only to the US Air Force and are offered for clarity.}

space assets. A generic term which may refer to any of the following individually or in combination: space systems, individual parts of a space system, space personnel, or supporting infrastructure. (AFDD 2-2)

space capability. 1. The ability of a space asset to accomplish a mission. 2. The ability of a terrestrial-based asset to accomplish a mission in space (e.g., a ground-based or airborne laser capable of negating a satellite). See also space; space asset. [JP 1-02] [*The ability of a space asset or system to accomplish a mission.*] [AFDD 2-2] {Words in brackets apply only to the Air Force and are offered for clarity.}

space control. Combat, combat support, and combat service support operations to ensure freedom of action in space for the United States and its allies and, when directed, deny an adversary freedom of action in space. The space control mission area includes: surveillance of space; protection of US and friendly space systems; prevention of an adversary's ability to use space systems and services for purposes hostile to US national security interests; negation of space systems and services used for purposes hostile to US national security interests; and directly supporting battle management, command, control, communications, and intelligence. (JP 1-02) [*Operations to attain and maintain a desired degree of space superiority by allowing friendly forces to exploit space capabilities while denying an adversaries ability to do the same (e.g. protection, prevention and negation). SC is achieved through offensive counterspace and defensive counterspace operations. Note: The Air Force uses counterspace as an equivalent definition of the space control mission.*] Also called **SC** (AFDD 2-2) {Words in brackets apply only to the US Air Force and are offered for clarity.}

space coordinating authority. An authority in theater to coordinate joint space operations and integrate space capabilities. SCA can be retained by the JFC but is generally delegated down to the functional component commander with the preponderance of space forces, expertise in space operations, and ability to command and control. (AFDD 2-2)

space forces. The space and terrestrial systems, equipment, facilities, organizations, and personnel necessary to access, use and, if directed, control space for national security. (JP 1-02) [*Operational military units which consist of some combination of space assets such as space-based and terrestrial equipment, facilities, organizations, and personnel used to exploit space for national security.*] [AFDD 2-2] {Words in brackets apply only to the Air Force and are offered for clarity.}

space force application. Combat operations in, through, and from space to influence the course and outcome of conflict. The space force application mission area includes ballistic missile defense and force projection. Also called **SFA** (JP 1-02)

space force enhancement. Combat support operations to improve the effectiveness of military forces as well as support other intelligence, civil, and commercial users. The space force enhancement mission area includes: ISR; integrated tactical warning and attack assessment; command, control, and communications; position, velocity, time, and navigation; and environmental monitoring. (JP 1-02) [*Space-based capabilities that contribute to maximizing the effectiveness of military air, land, sea and space operations as well as support other intelligence, civil, and commercial users. The SFE mission area includes: ISR; integrated warning and attack assessment; communications; positioning, navigation and timing; blue force tracking; space environment monitoring and weather services.*] Also called **SFE** (AFDD 2-2) {Words in brackets apply only to the US Air Force and are offered for clarity.}

space parity. That condition wherein neither opposing force enjoys an appreciable advantage over the other in controlling the space domain. (AFDD 2-2)

space situation awareness. The requisite current and predictive knowledge of space events, threats, activities, conditions, and space system (space, ground, link) status, capabilities, constraints and employment—current and future, friendly and hostile—to enable commanders, decision makers, planners, and operators to gain and maintain space superiority across the spectrum of conflict. Space situation awareness is the cornerstone of space operations, all-inclusive of space force enhancement, space support, and space control. Also called **SSA** (AFDD 2-2)

space superiority. The degree of dominance in space of one force over another that permits the conduct of operations by the former and its related land, sea, air, space, and special operations forces at a given time and place without prohibitive interference by the opposing force. (JP 1-02) [*That level of control in the space domain that one force enjoys over another that permits the conduct of operations at a given time and place without prohibitive interference by the opposing force. Space superiority may be localized in time and space, or it may be broad and enduring.*] (AFDD 2-2) {Words in brackets apply only to the Air Force and are offered for clarity.}

space support. Combat service support operations to deploy and sustain military and intelligence systems in space. The space support mission area includes launching and deploying space vehicles, maintaining and sustaining spacecraft on-orbit, and deorbiting and recovering space vehicles, if required. (JP 1-02) [*Those operations conducted with the objective of deploying, sustaining, and augmenting elements or capabilities of military space systems. Space support consists of spacelift, on-orbit support, deorbiting and recovering space vehicles, and reconstitution of space forces.* Also called **SS** (AFDD 2-2) {Words in brackets apply only to the US Air Force and are offered for clarity.}

space supremacy. That level of control in the space domain that one force enjoys over another that permits the conduct of operations at a given time and place without effective interference by the opposing force. Space supremacy may be localized in time and space, or it may be broad and enduring. (AFDD 2-2)

space system. A system with a major functional component that operates in the space environment or affects a space-based capability. Space systems consist of nodes and links. There are three nodes: space, terrestrial, and airborne. A space system also consists of links: control and mission. (AFDD 2-2)

www.ingramcontent.com/pod-product-compliance
Lightning Source LLC
Chambersburg PA
CBHW080535290526
45790CB00006B/2420